Bill Grossman

IN PURSUIT

Recollections
of a
Retired Colorado Game Warden

IN PURSUIT

*Recollections
of a
Retired Colorado Game Warden*

By

W. E. "BILL" GOOSMAN

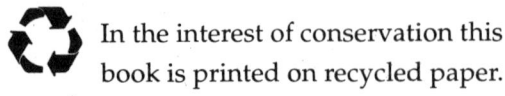 In the interest of conservation this book is printed on recycled paper.

DEDICATED

To

" SKIPPER"

WITH MY LOVE

ACKNOWLEDGMENTS

The dedication of this book to my wife, "Skipper", known to others as "Shirley", is in recognition of her untold patience and her understanding of my game warden duties which took away so much from my time at home. I owe her a deep measure of gratitude as she has continued to express her faith in me and has supported me in the writing of this book which records events in years of my life, most of which we have shared.

To Solveig Belland and "Buck" Benner, my sincere thanks for their efforts in doing research for me.

To the entire staff of Cook & Company I wish to express my sincere appreciation for the assistance given in bringing this book to reality. Mike has been generous with advice, suggestions and guidance, while Lisa has offered to proof read. In addition, without the professional expertise of Tonya Morris - the book would still be a ream of pages in a cardboard box! Lynn Carroll has joined the rest with words of encouragement which have been a significant bonus for my efforts. My thanks to all of you!

PHOTO & DESIGN CREDITS

The image of the elk used in this book is a reduction by Cook & Company of a photograph of my non-typical elk scoring 400 0/8 points in the Boone and Crockett records. The original photograph was taken by J. T. Washburn.

~ ~

The photograph of my talking on the two-way radio as I sat in my State pickup is a (then) Colorado Game and Fish Department photo taken by George D. Andrews.

~ ~

The cover design was created
By
Mike Cook

~ ~

All preliminary, ending and chapter page
designs are the creation of
Tonya Morris

FOREWORD

It has been said that Bill Goosman marches to a different drummer. Maybe. But, in any event, throughout over 53 years of marriage to him I have found that he is steadfast, and dedicated to any project which he undertakes.

At an early age he vowed that someday he would be a game warden; and so he was. In the processes that were to follow he has always met his challenges with vigor, never taking his obligations lightly.

Then, when he said that he was going to write a book as many had urged him to do, I knew that he would.

His hours of thought, recollections and references to diaries and journals have resulted in this chronicle of a significant period in his life, a life which I'm happy to have shared.

The original draft of this book is found in Big Chief tablets, spiral ringed notebooks and on yellow legal pads containing miles of words which Bill has written in longhand. All of these pages will be preserved as they represent a further testimonial to his steadfastness and his dedication to the completion of this autobiography.

To Bill: my compliments and - always my love.

- Shirley

INTRODUCTION

Following is an account of some of my experiences while I was a Colorado Game Warden, a title later changed to: "Wildlife Conservation Officer". In my mind, though, I was always a "game warden".

In some of the stories the names have been changed, and, on a few occasions, the identifying details have been disguised - all in an effort to protect the guilty.

With these exceptions aside, the contents of this book are based on facts relating to events which occurred as I continued "In Pursuit".

- The Author

PREFACE

As the author, I have some observations which may offer a more positive perspective to those who hold a view different from mine regarding the harvesting of game animals.

First, when an animal is killed it is expected that the meat will be well cared for and put to good use as a source of food. As a matter of fact, that is the law wherever I have hunted. So, the bulk of us hunters do not simply go out and slaughter - without any regard for the benefits that an animal might provide as sustenance.

Moreover, when hunters are in pursuit of a trophy they are seeking the older, more mature of the species. Those animals which have advanced beyond their prime without being harvested often become statistics through other circumstances which are less desirable to witness or imagine.

We who are true sportspersons serve a worthy purpose in the control of the populations and the conservation of the herds. In addition, our license dollars are used to a significant extent to support research and improvement of the quality of the wildlife which we all enjoy, and to preserve its habitat for future generations.

T R I B U T E

To the late Marie E. Potter, mother of the author's wife.

The Talking Books provided by the Library of Congress free of charge to the blind and those with limited eyesight gave many hours of pleasure.

The author has granted to the Library of Congress the right to provide Braille editions and special recordings of these works for the exclusive use of the blind and the physically handicapped. Therefore, a license is granted, through the Library of Congress, for such reproduction and distribution solely for the use of persons who are certified by competent authority as unable to read normal printed material as a result of their physical limitations.

Chapter One

I was born on November 7, 1919, eleven miles south of Hayden, Colorado, on a ranch that my father operated. I was the third of four children; my two sisters were older than I.

Soon after my brother was born my folks moved to their homestead about four miles farther on west. There we lived for several years, we kids growing up in a remote area. Of course, there was no electricity; no running water. (The only "running water" I knew of was when it rained!)

For a number of years after we moved to the homestead my mother was in poor health. Therefore, a neighbor lady assisted in taking care of us children and did a lot of the housework. She was very strict with us kids, and expected us to "toe the mark", so to speak. At this time I was around four years old.

Anyway, I did something she didn't approve of; so, I got a paddling. I waited until the time was right and then ran off to join my father who was repairing some fence several hundred yards beyond the cabin.

After I caught up with him and told him what had happened dad wiped the tears from my face and told me that I could stay with him and "help" him fix fence. Some time later, while stretching the wire, he spied a porcupine under a small bush. He always carried a .22 rifle to shoot porcupines, and rattlesnakes. This country was crawling with rattlers. After discovering the porcupine we edged up very close to it, and dad said that I could shoot it - with his help.

I had never fired a gun at that tender age; so he held the rifle and told me to pull the trigger. I did - and with one loud "bang" the porky flattened out. (Little did I know at the time that a slap from a porcupine's tail could result in a nosefull of quills for a dog, horse or cow.)

Anyway I received my introduction to firearms when I was quite young. At the age of six I was doing a lot of shooting with a .22 rifle. My dad was a crack shot with both a .22 rifle and a shotgun. I never knew of him firing a big rifle, however.

I've hunted all my life and although I'm past 78 years old now, I still hunt anytime I can. I've hunted big game in several of the states, including Hawaii, and in Canada. Even in Australia and New Guinea there were a few occasions when I got to hunt, though most of my targets were in the sights of a .50 caliber machine gun from the blister of a Catalina flying boat. Among my trophies on the wall, however, are the grand slam of bighorn sheep as well as other big game animals with several making the Boone and Crockett records.

When I was 17 I took a job as trail boss with the U.S. Forest Service, building trails in the Lost Lakes area. This job lasted through the summer of 1937, terminating on September 1st. It was then that I contacted the Colorado Game and Fish Department, applying for a job as a beaver trapper or a game warden. I felt certain that I could handle either job. I'd trapped lots of beaver, and since the age of 14 I'd guided deer and elk hunters. All of this entailed a good deal of "horse sense", experience in packing, and a first-hand knowledge of wildlife and its habits. (My dad had often said that he thought I'd cut my teeth on a gun barrel and an elk bone.)

My application reached the Denver office, and I was given the "nod" for an interview, which responsibility was to fall on the shoulders of George Steele, game warden in charge of the Hot Sulphur Springs district.

After submitting my application I had left on a pack trip into the Lost Lakes vicinity, looking for an area to take elk hunters come October. In my application I'd given my address as Hayden, Colorado; so that's where George Steele came to interview me, all decked out in full Game and Fish Department uniform.

According to what George told me later, he spent most of the day in and around Hayden looking for me. He said that whenever he asked anyone about me they would say, "Yes, I know Bill; but I don't know where you could find him now." Finally, toward evening he asked an old friend of mine where he might find me. The friend cautiously asked why

George was looking for me, to which George replied that I had made an application for a job with the Game Department. He said that I was as good as hired; but that there were some papers to be filled out. My friend said, "Well, why in the hell didn't you SAY why you wanted to find him?" Everyone had thought that George wanted to pinch me for something.

Arriving back in Hayden I learned of George's visit, and a few days later I received a letter from a Mr. John Hart, the Assistant Director of the Game and Fish Department. He advised me that if I would appear before him at the Denver office probably I would be given a job; and, I would have to fill out some papers.

Needless to say, I didn't waste much time rounding up a close friend of mine to go to Denver with me. The thought of driving through Denver to the State Capitol Building was terrifying to two young bucks from the boondocks. I'd much rather have stepped up on a raw bronc than to have driven through the "heavy" Denver traffic!

After my meeting with Mr. Hart I was informed that I was hired, and was to report to Mr. George Steele at Hot Sulphur Springs. My duties began on November 1, 1937, when I was employed at a wage of $75.00 per month. I had to furnish my own transportation and pay any expense I might have. I would be 18 on the 7th of that month.

I don't remember that Mr. Hart asked me how old I was, but as long as I could catch beaver and knew something about game - I could learn the rest. He gave me a summons book, a couple of notebooks to keep a record of my activities in and a badge. In parting he offered some fatherly advice.

Chapter Two

Until the freeze-up I trapped beaver in the Hot Sulphur Springs district. At that time no one could trap beaver legally without a permit from the Game Department, and those permits were hard to get. Also, they were quite limited as to the number of beaver allowed on each permit.

By the time it had frozen up too much for good beaver trapping the heavy snows had driven most of the elk and deer out of the high country to lower areas which caused them to move in on private property. The elk started working on the haystacks in the Hot Sulphur-Kremmling areas and a lot of deer concentrated along the river bottoms and on the railroad rights-of-way.

In those days the Game Department had established feed yards for both deer and elk. One of them for elk was located just west of Byers Canyon on the south side of the river from Highway 40. The other was up the Troublesome River north of Kremmling. The one for deer was west of Byers Canyon on the north side of Highway 40.

On the first yard mentioned there were 421 head of elk coming in to that yard nightly. I fed them between 18 and 24 bales of hay each day, depending on the weather. There was a stack yard nearby with two stacks of hay. The stack yard fence consisted of a four barbed wire stock fence such as used as a property fence. Although the elk went by this stack yard daily to and from their bedding area, not once did an elk jump into the stack yard.

I lost only one elk throughout the winter on their two feed yards, and one buck died on the deer feed yard. The deer had been wounded, apparently during the past hunting season.

That winter I learned a lot about feeding both elk and deer. The secret to feeding deer is to not over-feed them so they will still browse around in the brush during the day. They have to have browse in their food chain to be healthy. If they are fed too much on the yard they won't have the desire to browse sometime through the day. Elk are a lot like cattle and will thrive on just hay as was proven by captive elk on the ranch where I grew up. The fact that I lost only one elk on the yards proved that elk can and will adjust to artificial feeding when done properly.

Over the years I proved beyond any doubt of the non-believers that my method of feeding elk was successful. Wyoming has for many years fed thousands of elk on their Jackson feed yards with excellent results.

As I've said, during the winter the deer would gather along the railroad tracks, there being less snow to travel, and there were bare banks where there might be a little feed. Another of my duties along with feeding at the three feed yards was running the deer off the tracks on foot, between Byers Canyon and Kremmling. If they weren't run off the trains might plow into them and scatter deerburgers all over the place. One such incident a year before had killed at least nineteen head. The elk didn't give us any trouble this way, however.

Not long after I settled in Hot Sulphur Springs I heard of a young man about my age who was referred to as "Tarzan of Williams Fork". The stories about this guy being a "super" man and an athlete with stamina that would put a bull elk to shame were told repeatedly in the area. Needless to say, I was anxious to see this "Superman".

One evening I pulled into a filling station run by Don Buckheister, to fill up my pickup tank for the night runs of deer and elk herding. Just then a young person with a very unusual physique walked in front of my pickup and went on into the station. As Don stuck the gas nozzle into the gas tank he saw me looking in the direction of the fellow mentioned. He filled the tank, hung the nozzle up and as we walked to the door of the station he asked me if I'd ever met Tommy Roberts. I said not that I could ever remember; so Don introduced me to one Tommy Roberts. When I shook hands with this guy it reminded me of the grip of a 4 1/2 Newhouse wolf trap. He had a rather handsome face and long blond hair that came down to his very broad shoulders. I would judge his height to be about 5'10". His arms and legs were powerfully built.

During my stay in Hot Sulphur I heard quite a bit about this man. The ranch on which he lived was located 18 miles south of Hot Sulphur. I had it proven to me that in fact he could dog-trot the distance from the ranch to Hot Sulphur, play a game of basketball and dog-trot all the way home.

The next time I ran into Tommy was in New Guinea during World War II. I was flying in an air-sea rescue Catalina and he was flying a P-38 Fighter. He was considered a top pilot and I might say a "dare devil" one at that. The last I heard of him was that his squadron had gone on a mission and had intercepted a large group of Jap fighters. It was reported that Tommy was one of the Americans shot down.

One day during the winter that I was in Hot Sulphur George Steele called me and said that he would like for me to drop by his house as he wanted to discuss a matter with me. After I finished getting hay out on the feed yards I swung by Steele's house. George said that he had received a complaint from a rancher on the Troublesome River about a small group of bull elk really raising hell with his hay stacks. He thought if we were to kill two or three it might cause the others to leave. Hanging lanterns on the stack yards and shooting at the elk with a 12-gauge shotgun hadn't bothered them so I doubted killing some of them would make much of a difference; but as far as I was concerned we might as well try it and see what happened.

After making my run on the railroad to scare the

deer off the tracks ahead of the next train I headed by George's home to pick him up to go after the bulls. He was waiting for me and all ready to go, except he didn't have a rifle. When I asked him where his rifle was he replied, "You are supposed to be a crack shot and you will do the shooting; so I won't take a rifle." I considered that quite a compliment.

This was a beautiful night with a nearly full moon. I assumed that we could drive right to the stack yard so I could use my spotlights to shoot by. We then headed for the Troublesome River area. After reaching the river road we drove on up it for several miles. It was really pretty out with the moon shining on the snow and reflecting millions of diamonds. George told me to turn off on the next road to our right. As soon as I saw the turnoff I knew we were in trouble as it was a sled road that led out into a field. My pickup was 2-wheel drive and I didn't have chains on. At that time I didn't know about 4-wheel drive. George said, "Ah, we can make it as the stack yard is just on the other side of a little creek that follows the willows running close to the stack yard." We didn't go far until the pickup slid off the sled track and we were stuck.

Since we were stuck and were several hundred yards from the stacks there was no way I could use my spotlights to shoot with. In those days I used a peep sight, not knowing anything about telescope sights. We followed the sled road to the creek which was frozen over. At this point George stopped and whispered that beyond the willows was the stack yard where the elk should be. We stepped clear of the willows and, sure enough, there were five bull elk standing in line getting ready to jump out of the stack yard. As soon as George saw the elk he whispered, "Shoot, shoot!", and slapped me on the back. The bulls jumped out of the yard and stopped. All of them looked like six-pointers. I tried to see my sights but couldn't, so I raised the rifle up until it was pointed at the moon. Then I could see my sights O.K. and I centered the front bead in the peep ring, bringing the rifle back down until the sights blurred with the lead bull.

When I thought the rifle was lined up about right for the lungs I squeezed the trigger. I heard the bullet hit with a thud, and the bulls all ran behind the stacks and out of sight from us. As I slammed another round into the chamber I heard George say, "I think you hit one." About this time four of the bulls ran out from behind the stacks and headed straight away from us. George was jumping up and down wanting me to shoot another one. I told him that I couldn't see my sights well enough and would probably hit one in the butt if I did shoot while they were running away from us. If I did that I knew that I would have to spend the next day on snowshoes running the bull down and finishing it off. Then I said, "Let's walk around the stacks and see where that fifth bull went."

When we got to where we could see behind the stacks, there lay the other bull - a seven pointer. Upon gutting it out I found that the bullet had entered the chest just back of the right shoulder and had even taken a tip of the heart off; but didn't go out the left side. I was pretty proud of that shot. I looked at my watch and it showed five minutes 'til midnight.

(A seven-point bull elk is identified as an Imperial. A six-point is a Royal, and an eight-point is a Monarch, as well he should be!)

In the morning I would ask the rancher to help me get the elk out to my pickup. In the meantime, we had to get my pickup "un-stuck" and back on the road. I still had two trains coming through between now and daylight. There were bound to be a lot of deer on the tracks and if I didn't get them off - the trains might. So, after shoveling back to the main road I had the pickup headed to town. I took George home and returned to my deer herding.

Incidentally, shooting the one bull elk at midnight on the Troublesome River ranch didn't stop the rest of the bulls from raiding the rancher's haystacks; just as I thought.

April rolled around and the deep snow was melting enough for the deer and elk to pull out for the upper country.

Chapter Three

In the spring of 1938, I received orders from the Denver office to report to Jim Campbell, Moffat County district warden stationed in Craig, Colorado. Although I'd never met him in person, I certainly knew who he was. (When I was a little boy the lady who cared for my brother and me when mother was ill used to tell us if we didn't behave ourselves she would "call Jim Campbell" and he would "get" us.) I still remember how this threat would shape up us boys.

Jim was a six-footer and weighed around 185 pounds. He had a big gray longhorn mustache and a booming voice. Being hard of hearing he would get up close to talk to you; consequently you never had to say, "Huh?" or ask him to repeat himself.

Jim was well respected throughout his area; but most people who had any reason to know were aware of Jim's routine patrol, and some took advantage of this knowledge. Part of my duties while in the Craig district would be to change this custom by patrolling where and when least expected.

After working with Jim for several months I became well acquainted with both him and his wife, Mary. Then I told them how the lady who cared for us boys was able to keep us in line. Jim had a good laugh out of that and afterwards when Mary wanted to poke a little fun at Jim she would call him the "bogey-man" and ask him how many little boys he had frightened that day.

I found Jim and Mary to be very kind people, and they treated me more like a son than an employee working under Jim. A fair sized book could be written on this big Scotsman's life adventures.

The summer passed and the big game hunting season came and went with nothing really outstanding. The snows settled in and Old Man Winter was here to stay for several months.

One evening along about mid-December I received a call from the boss in Denver. He wanted me to close up my apartment where I had been batching, and - if at all possible - to meet him at the Denver office the following evening. I told him that the passes (Rabbit Ears and Berthoud) were in bad shape, and that Rabbit Ears had been closed the day before. He then gave me orders to go through Wyoming and to be prepared to stay for at least six weeks. He wanted me to bring my big rifle, a .22 caliber rifle and a heavy six-shooter. He didn't tell me what kind of assignment I was in for over the phone; he said that

I'd find out when I arrived in Denver. He said that he would wait for me until midnight.

I arrived at the Denver office at about 6:00 p.m. and at this point met Mr. John Hart, the boss man, and another game warden, Bill Forgett from Evergreen.

I soon found out that Bill and I were to work together in Colorado Springs, doing deer control work in and around that area where the deer were raising hell with the shrubbery and plants in people's yards. Since it was absolutely impossible to open a "Post" season to relieve the problem, the Game and Fish Department had to resort to control killing. The meat was always donated to charitable institutions and hospitals.

The boss wanted us to use .22 rifles if at all possible, and switch to big rifles only if the .22 rim fire didn't do the job. He then asked us what we thought. Bill Forgett didn't have anything to say about it, so I sounded off, telling the boss that it wouldn't work. Too many deer would be wounded and we'd spend most of our time running down cripples. He still wanted us to try the .22 rim fire first, and if that didn't work out, then go to the center fire, or big rifles. For the big rifle I'd decided to use my .220 Swift; Bill had a .270 Winchester.

By noon the following day we had our ammo rounded up and a room reserved at a Colorado Springs motel. We'd also made arrangements with the Colorado Springs locker plant to accept any and all of the deer brought in to them. The game warden stationed in the Springs would do the hauling of the carcasses.

By evening we were settled in our motel room

and were going over matters concerning the upcoming control work when the phone rang. Bill answered. As he listened to the caller's conversation he turned around and stared at me with a perplexed look on his face, then he spoke into the phone, "The hell they did!!!" For the next few minutes he shifted from one foot to the other, and every so often would mutter, "Uh-huh... yes, Mam... well... I'll be...... darned!".... .several times. Then he repeated an address and said that we would be right over.

When he hung up the receiver I asked what that was all about. He looked at me with a thoughtful expression and then said, "This lady says that two big bucks have knocked over the Wise Men and have eaten Christ out of the manger!" I responded, "What in the hell are you talking about, fella?" Bill then explained that a Mrs. So-and-So had set up a very elaborate Christmas display of the Christ-child in the manger and with some Wise Men and sheep. She had used real hay in the manger and this had attracted the two big bucks.

This was the night of December 20th, and the third time her display had been turned upside down. She had just called the boss in Denver and wanted something done about it. Mr. Hart had told her that two wardens were in Colorado Springs right then to take care of such matters and told her where she could contact us, and to call immediately.

Since Bill had her address we decided to drive by and look the situation over. Bill was driving a 1935 model sedan with three spotlights mounted on it; so we decided to take it as we would have plenty of lights to use. He suggested that I take my rifle along in case we got a chance to shoot one of the bucks. It was agreed that, under these circumstances, we'd better consider the big rifle. So I would take my .220 that shot a 48 grain bullet with a velocity of 4140 feet per second. It was an excellent caliber for this kind of shooting due to the high velocity and a very small bullet. This round seldom completely penetrated a deer's carcass; therefore, there was small chance of it exiting and doing unwanted damage down range.

When we arrived at the lady's estate, sure enough, there were two big four-point bucks putting the finishing touches on the already shambles of what earlier had been a beautiful Christmas display. We drove by slowly and sized up the situation. Beyond the buildings we found where the deer has been crossing the road from the brushy side and jumping a four-foot fence into the estate.

We concluded that if we worked it right we could get the bucks to spook out of the estate area along the same route they had used to get into it.

Bill asked me if I thought I could shoot one or both if he could run them by me. I agreed to give it a try and see what happened. We decided that Bill was to be dropped off back beyond the scene of the damage and I would drive on to where I could cover the exit point of the bucks. I dropped Bill off, then drove on to the other side of the buildings.

I turned two of the spotlights on the trail and the point where the deer had jumped into the property - and - got ready. I no sooner did this until the two bucks came bounding around the corner of the buildings, headed for the fence that was lit by one of the spotlights. As the leader of the two made a jump to clear the fence I touched off the .220. The shot connected with the buck at the height of his jump and he hit the ground like a sack of mush. The second buck had cleared the fence and was about to take his first jump across the road when I squeezed a shot off for his neck. The buck folded up and slid to the center of the road as dead as a door nail. About this time Bill showed up, hot on the trail of the two bucks. When he saw both bucks piled up he said, "From now on I'm going to call you 'Buckskin Bill'."

In the next two weeks I shot 87 more deer with only two requiring two shots each to put them down for good. The longest shot was stepped off by Bill at 341 steps.

After we wound up the control work on deer at Colorado Springs we returned to Evergreen where I worked on elk control for the rest of the winter. This was decided by the Denver boss since Bill had a lot of duties besides elk control and I didn't have anything elsewhere that required my immediate attention.

Chapter Four

At the time I was assigned to elk control work in the Evergreen area, as mentioned earlier, the Game Department could not open a post season to relieve damage caused by big game animals. Therefore, control shooting was the last resort.

A lot of the elk had migrated into the Evergreen area by this time of year and were using up the available food supply. The only solution to the matter was control shooting.

As this was Bill's district he was in charge of it, and my responsibility was shooting elk anywhere in Bill's area that I might find them. I would gut them and at the end of the day I would report their location to a man (Art) who was hired to get the elk out and hauled to the Evergreen locker plant. Art knew this area inside and out; therefore, he was able to find all of the elk I killed. He had a Diamond-T truck with solid rubber tires. On this monster he had a hefty winch mounted so he could hoist the elk right up onto the truck bed.

I was located in Evergreen for about three months. During this time I killed a lot of elk scattered around the Evergreen area. I never had to tell Art twice where each elk was; he gathered them all up. Again, the meat was donated to some charitable institution or to hospitals in the area, Denver included.

To start with, I loved to hunt, and especially elk; however, this was THE longest hunt I was ever on. Of all the elk I shot during these three months I never shot a cow that was old enough to bear a calf in the spring.

At the start of this control shooting I began using a Model 70 Winchester in .220 Swift caliber. I had used this rifle on deer and elk for several years and had excellent results with it; however, one morning soon after starting the control hunting I cut the tracks of two bulls made in the light snow that fell during the night. I soon tracked the bulls to a small clearing. One was following the other about 160 yards away. They were getting close to the timber so I instantly dropped to a sitting position intending to shoot the leader through the lungs (my favorite shot on big game). I squeezed the trigger and heard the bullet hit. The bull went down as if his legs had been jerked out from under him.

The second bull hesitated just before entering the timber. I swung on him and touched 'er off. I heard the "thunk" as the bullet hit and the bull went out of sight into the timber. I slipped a couple of rounds into the magazine and headed for the bulls. Part of the distance I had to cover led through some trees and out of sight of the elk. They were both average six-pointers.

When I came into sight of the park I couldn't see either bull. I found a few drops of blood where the first bull had fallen and saw his tracks leading out into the timber. I figured he had mustered a surge of strength, gotten up and gone into the bush aways before falling for good. I looked for bull #2 and found him lying a little ways into the timber. I gutted this one out, then took up the trail for the other one.

I trailed this bull until almost dark without even jumping him and never saw much blood; so I decided that he wasn't hurt too badly. I figured that I had just creased him somehow, because if he had been shot through the lungs he wouldn't have gone over a hundred yards at most. This was the last elk hunt that I ever used the .220 on. I switched to my .300 H&H Mag. with 180 grain bullets for the balance of my control work.

About two weeks later I shot a six-point bull in this area. Upon gutting him I discovered that he had been shot recently. The bullet had entered his chest area back of the shoulder and just under the backbone. It didn't hit a rib going in or out, and showed only a small bruise on the bottom of the backbone. This would have been completely healed up in another two weeks. When a bullet passes through this area and doesn't hit bone in or out it doesn't expand, thereby not causing any other damage. It may have hit a nerve under the backbone causing the bull to hit the ground but in a jiffy be back on his feet making tracks out of there. Anyway, I didn't use the .220 anymore.

I killed quite a number of elk on the Evergreen control work and only four head took more than one shot to get them down. I am a strong believer of placing your shot where it will do the most good. Later on I changed to a 7mm Remington Magnum in a Winchester Model 70 rifle. Up to the time this is written I have made forty-two one-shot kills on big game from pronghorn antelope through grizzly.

One day while on my Evergreen elk control assignment I found myself sitting on a high point where I could see a lot of the surrounding area. I decided that this would be a good time and place to eat the candy bar which comprised my lunch. Also, I might locate some elk from this point. While sitting there in the warm sun I began re-living some of my life and the circumstances leading up to my present employment.

I remembered quite vividly that when I was about nine years old my folks lived on a big ranch in the Williams Fork area. My dad was the foreman for the ranch owner. In those days there were lots of sage chickens in that country and just about everyone ate them in one form or another. Of course, my folks never wasted any food item, so my mother utilized the old roosters by grinding the meat and making "chickenburgers" out of them. As I recall they were very good.

Since my dad never learned to drive we didn't have an automobile. Our only methods of transportation were either by wagon or saddle horse. Due to this we didn't get to town very often. The ranch owner had an early model Chevrolet pickup and occasionally when he was going to Hayden or Craig he would take my brother or me with him.

One day in August he was going to Craig and asked if I wanted to go along if it was okay with my mother. It was, so we headed to Craig. The route he took would lead us across a big high mesa that was a grain field bordered by thick sagebrush.

As we drove across this bench, or mesa, we encountered a small flock of sage chickens. It so happened that they were feeding toward the bordering sage brush on the left side of the road. They were all roosters as far as I could tell, and all big ones, too. As we got almost even with the chickens the rancher stopped, grabbed a .22 rifle from the hooks behind the seat, laid the rifle out the window and proceeded to shoot one of the sage chickens. In rapid succession he shot nine chickens before the rest of them flew off. At this point I jerked my door open with the thought of going after the chickens. (In the past, from the time I was big enough, I'd become the so-called "retriever" for my dad. When he shot and I saw something fall I didn't waste any time going after that chicken or rabbit.)

"Hey, where you goin'...don't bother with them damned old chickens; they ain't no good to eat." I explained to him that I could take them home and my mother would make chickenburgers out of them. He told me again to forget the old roosters and started the pickup. At my age I couldn't argue with him and besides, I was afraid he would drive off without me and I'd have to walk home. So, I got in, and when I asked him why he did that he said, "The reason I shot them is because they eat a lot of my grain before it is cut." That did it. From there on to Craig and back I didn't do much talking although I did a lot of thinking. Kid-like, I vowed that someday I would be a game warden and pinch that old boy for shooting the chickens and leaving them lie there.

After my elk control duties in Evergreen were over I was assigned again to the Craig district to work under Jim Campbell. One day my patrol was up the Williams Fork River. When I reached the Pagoda store I stopped in to buy a candy bar and get a cup of coffee. I knew the owner quite well and he asked me who I had pinched lately. I replied, "Nobody yet today; but I'm lookin'." He got over close to me out of earshot of others in the store and said in a low voice, "Why don't you drive up South Fork and watch the Pagoda Creek area. It might be worth your time."

I thanked him for the information, paid for the coffee and candy bar and then drove up the South Fork to the Pagoda Creek road. From there I went up some tracks to where a horse trail came down off the mountain. I could see that several horses had gone up this trail sometime that day. I knew from experience that this trail led to the high country and, of course, to the summer range of the elk herd in this area. All of this country was quite familiar to me since I'd trapped it while growing up on the ranch near Pagoda.

After thinking the matter over I decided to drive on up the tracks, or road, to get away from the trail, and intercept the horsebackers when they came out. By the time I got situated it was after 2:00 o'clock. I waited until late evening and then decided they had gone out another way.

Several days later I stopped in at a bar in Craig at about 9:00 p.m. to see what I could learn about any poaching action in the area. A man that I had known for several years in Hayden came in. When he saw me he came over and shook hands, then said, "Let's get a booth and have a beer." After we were seated, and seeing that no one else was close by he said, "Bill, I've got some dope you might be interested in." Coming from him I figured that it would be "interesting" to hear; so I said, "Shoot, I'm listening."

He then asked me if I'd been up to the Pagoda Creek trail a few days ago, and if I'd waited for some horsebackers to come out on that trail. I said that I had, but no one showed up while I was waiting. He told me that the owner of the ranch where I grew up and one of his hired hands had gone up in that area and shot a spike bull, planning to bring it out that evening. However, before riding out to the mouth of the trail they had found a high point where they could see about a mile up the road, or tracks, to where I was waiting. They had binoculars and upon seeing the pickup they recognized it as mine. As a consequence they didn't come out until around 11:00 p.m. that night. My informant's wife had heard these details from the hired man's wife.

So, after all of this time I had almost accomplished my vow: to become a game warden and to pinch the "old boy" who had shot those nine sage chicken roosters and left them there to be wasted.

However, upon searching the premises, I didn't find the elk. (Later, I found out that I should have dug deeper into the grain bin in the barn!)

In any event, "Farmer's Season" closed for a while.

Chapter Five

When World War II broke out I enlisted in the Army Air Corps in January, 1942. During the next two weeks at a "retreat" in Texas they tried to teach me to march. (My snowshoe stride played hell with keeping in step, though!) Then, I was given a free train ride to Boston and, twenty-three days after joining up, in February, I boarded the Queen Mary where I sailed for forty days and forty nights to arrive in Melbourne, Australia.

(When we'd reached the Panama Canal - where we were to have taken a "short-cut" back into the Pacific - we were told "they" had discovered that the Queen Mary was too large to navigate the locks! So, we "backed 'er up" - and landed, briefly, in Rio de

Janeiro.) Looked GOOD to me!...as it did to quite a few of the other ten thousand troops on board. Some of the enlisted men jumped ship, headed for the bright lights. Then - lower ranking officers were sent to gather up all of the swimmers. Eventually, higher ranking personnel went ashore trying to collect all of the sight-seers. Finally, though, it was concluded that too many Good and Honest Men were NOT inclined to continue on our ocean voyage; so we headed East - without them.

Just as we were exiting the corridor from the harbor into the open Atlantic waters a tanker steamed by us. Not long afterwards KA-BLEW-EEE!! No more tanker! From that point on our trip was "dipsy-doodle", changing course every seven minutes in an effort to avoid the lurking submarines.

I never was a sea-goer; didn't have the sickness that some did; but, Boy! I sure couldn't ride a hammock!...so I would sneak up on deck, find a hideout and try to catch a few winks before some guard discovered me. Finally, I had a buddy with "poor eyesight" and was THAT ever appreciated!

Eventually we hit Cape Town, Africa...spent a little time there and then headed into the Indian Ocean. I was supposed to go to Burma, but a heavy sea battle changed all of those plans, and - at last - I was in Melbourne. We'd been around the world to reach this destination!

It wasn't too long before I was sent to New Guinea where I joined an Air-Sea Rescue crew on a Catalina flying boat as the left-hand waist gunner. This involved the use of a .50 caliber machine gun and, I might say, it was very impressive. It would tear a zero fighter to pieces in short order. It also made a good gun for shark-hunting - a control measure for the sake of any downed airmen.

My ability to use a gun well got me out of several tight spots over there during the next few years.

I came home with the Distinguished Flying Cross, the Air Medal with three Oak Leaf Clusters, among other citations — along with a bad leg and a mean case of malaria.

After the war I wound up with the Colorado Game and Fish Department again, and was assigned to the Meeker district, which, then, included all of Rio Blanco County and fringe areas of all of the adjacent counties. I was to replace Cleve Gentry who had been the game warden in this district for many years. Now Cleve had been promoted to District Chief Warden and his area would cover five counties. There was not enough time to take care of all of these new duties and those of the district warden too. Cleve would be my immediate supervisor. He was known and respected far and wide; it would be quite a job to fill his boots!

Now married, we had just built a new home in Denver; we'd lived in it only four months when I received my appointment and orders to locate in Meeker. So, in January of 1947, we moved west - lock, stock and barrel.

Through Cleve we'd spoken for an apartment but when we arrived it was still occupied. That meant find another place to live for a few days. The only available housing was in a one-room log cabin. Our truck-load of furniture had taken a wrong turn in the meantime, ending up in Breckenridge! When it did finally arrive we found storage in Gentry's basement since it sure wasn't going to fit in our present quarters!

This was a far cry from modern accommodations, and took some getting used to. There was a little coal-wood stove in one corner and a table that hinged up to a wall-niche serving as a "cupboard". (The table had to be raised, of course, in order to get to the bed which occupied the north wall.) The remaining space was allotted to the rest of the furniture: two straight-backed chairs, a metal clothes closet and the stand holding the wash basin and water bucket above which was a shelf for dishes. The "bath" was down the path.

Our next door neighbors were two brothers who were "Gung-Ho" for porcupines - not live ones, but for eating. There were countless thousands of these four-legged "pin cushions" and the boys were trying to keep 'em in check by eating the surplus.

One day I asked them why they ate porcupine meat. One of them spoke up and said, "Well, there ain't no season on 'em so we don't have to worry about the game warden gettin' us. Then, they're easy to come by and we just kinda like 'em. All they cost us is one .22 bullet, so ya' can't go wrong with that." I didn't pursue the matter further, but decided that they were welcome to their fried "quill pig". I'd stick to elk, beef and pork.

During the days that we were "entrenched" in this "motel" it snowed often - and the wind blew - from the north. As a result, several mornings when we woke up there would be little snowdrifts on the covers after the snow had blown through the cracks in the logs. By the time we left we had most of those cracks plugged up, however. This was our initiation to Meeker.

My first patrol in my new district was down

Piceance Creek. I looked at the scenery so much - and the deer seen on this trip — that I had a very sore neck from it. Ducking down, looking up through the windshield at the tops of the hills was the probable reason for my stiffness. I drove this route thousands of times over the following number of years and I always enjoyed it. Usually I saw something new that I hadn't seen before.

And then, there was Rangely, a town located in the western end of Rio Blanco County, about sixty-three miles from Meeker. In the Forties it was an oil boom town, and brought in lots of transient workers - many with a distinct taste for venison, regardless of the time of year.

To demonstrate: early on I made a patrol down to the west end of my district intending to look the area over, and to see what changes had resulted from the oil boom. I didn't quite get into the Rangely city limits when I was bogged down in a huge mud hole...stuck! After having to be pulled out backwards by one of the highway trucks working on this mess, I decided to head back to Meeker and make my entrance into Rangely under better road conditions. I knew full well that the word would soon be out that the new game warden had started into town, got stuck, and turned back. No one would know for sure what I'd intended to do if I had gone on into town, though.

Two days later, after highway workers had repaired the road damage I made a return trip to Rangely. After lunch I went out to the city dump, expecting to find one or two pieces of venison. But - nothing like I DID find! All together I counted twenty-one pieces of deer meat; most were quarters.

Apparently some of the poachers got a little shook up over news of my previous trip and decided that it was time for them to make trips to the dump, too, just in case I planned on searching someone.

Chapter Six

A major portion of the high country in my district was accessible only by foot or horseback. As a result I bought myself a saddle horse and a good strong pack horse. While I gathered up all of the necessary tack and equipment the Department kicked in with a two-horse trailer. Now I was prepared to patrol those remote areas.

I spent a lot of time patrolling the high country for hunters and fishermen at the high lakes. My pack horse, Kit, didn't have to be led; she would follow my saddle horse, Sally, a little bay mare that never forgot where she had gone before. Sometimes I would ride an. area where there was no trail; I would just cut across country to reach a certain place that I wanted to check. A short-cut was sometimes rougher going than following a trail, but, it was usually quicker.

One particular time I pulled my horse up to the Hill Creek campground as I wanted to check for elk at and around the headwaters of the creek. About a year before I had gone up this way and found a high knob where I had a bird's eye view for miles around. For about 250 yards it was quite a steep approach; but if I slabbed around to get to the top it made the climb much easier. The only trouble with that was a big ponderosa pine that grew on the hillside and had a huge limb that stuck out on the downhill side. Upon riding past or under this limb a person had to duck real low - or - be swept out of the saddle.

This day, just before I got to the pine, I saw a red fox jump up from behind a bush and run down over the hill to my right. To watch him I had to turn around a little in the saddle - and - I knew that I was getting pretty close to the pine tree and its limb. As Sally quickened her step to get up the sharp incline from the tree to the top, it flashed through my mind to look out for the limb! I spun around in the saddle and saw that it was too late to duck under the limb.

The only thing left for me to do was kick my feet out of the stirrups and slide off the back of the horse. Things happened so fast that - I forgot to turn loose of the reins! As I felt the horse start to rear up I realized that I was still holding onto the reins and was about to pull her over on top of me. I released the reins and rolled on over backwards. I could almost feel Sally coming on over backwards too and landing right in my middle. I hit the ground rolling and tried to keep rolling even faster. After about the second roll I saw that Sally had gotten her front feet back on the ground and was just standing there.

After I stopped tumbling around I checked for possible broken bones and finding none then checked my horse and found that there was nothing wrong with her; so started brushing off the dirt. It was then that I discovered I'd lost my six-shooter; later I found it lying under a bush.

Everything turned out O.K. and I finished my ride; but I couldn't help thinking what might have happened if my horse had fallen over on me. That could have messed things up for good.

Many times when I was patrolling the Flat Tops area by horseback I would be gone for up to five days before returning to my pickup. A lot of this time was checking on elk hunters who had packed in anywhere from three to five days before season opened. Some of them would "jump the gun" and open season several days early. By opening morning they would have their elk and would pack it out opening day. After two or three years of hitting these high-country camps and issuing a few summonses for violating the laws I put a stop to a good deal of the early hunting.

For example: one fall I set my goal to bust up a camp of early elk hunters who would pack into the Marvine Peak area and get their elk before season opened. They made it a habit to wait, however, until the second day of season to start packing out, assuming that there was little chance of a game warden spotting an early kill.

During the summer I had located their camp site according to information I had received. Other hunters who also camped in the same general area didn't appreciate these guys hunting two or three days before season; so they talked to me about it.

I owned some land on South Fork at the mouth of Lost Solar Creek. It had a one-room cabin on it which worked real well for a patrol station in conjunction with checking the Flat Tops area.

This particular fall I packed up the South Fork to my cabin ahead of opening day of the elk season. I had a friend who was a biologist for the Department and had spent the summer working with the elk in this area. Jack Devore knew what I intended to do and wanted to ride along. I was glad to have him as he would be company as well as a good witness - and extra help - in case I found illegal game in the camp I had in mind.

We were up at 4:00 a.m. the day before season, ate our breakfast, stowed lunches in our saddle bags and were ready to ride at the crack of dawn. As we swung up the Lost Solar Creek trail a light snow started falling and it looked like it could do nothing but get worse throughout the day.

About three miles up Lost Solar Creek we found an elk camp with no one around. The hunters had gone up the trail ahead of us as indicated by two fresh sets of horse tracks. They had left three horses in camp, two of which were tied to trees and the third had a picket rope that was tied to the base of a ten-foot high pine tree. This tree was on the side-hill, but the rope wasn't long enough to permit the horse to reach level ground. The ground was already wet and there were about four inches of snow on top of this. It looked like the horse had tried to follow the riders and had circled around another smaller pine. At this point the picket rope got hung up and the horse had fallen and couldn't get up. He had his back downhill and was in bad shape. Certainly he would have died long before the hunters returned. I cut the picket rope to get the horse up, and tied him to a good, sound tree close to the tent.

From there we rode on up Lost Solar to the head of Park Creek. By this time the light snow we had started out in was turning into a blizzard out on top. The snow was knee-deep to our horses and the farther we went the worse the storm became. The horses were to the point that they didn't want to face it anymore; so after considering everything I concluded that it was foolish to continue. I told Jack that we were going to turn back. He sure didn't veto the idea; so we rode back to the timber where we had some shelter, built a fire and ate a late lunch while we warmed up a little.

Time, then, to head back down Lost Solar Creek and toward camp. When we reached the elk camp lower down Lost Solar around 3:30 p.m. the two hunters had returned to camp and were just leaving again with their rifles - headed up the trail. As we rode up they stepped out of the trail. We stopped and I asked them if they were the hunters from that camp. One of them said that they were. I then told them about finding one of their horses down, that we'd cut it loose and tied it up so it couldn't get into trouble again. One of the guys said, "Thanks a lot; we knew something had happened when we found him tied up close to the tent." He continued, "By the way, did you guys do any good today?" Jack and I both had rifles on our saddles and apparently he thought we were hunting.

I told him that we hadn't done any good yet, but things were looking better. (At that time it was illegal to carry a rifle out of camp for three days before season opened.) Jack and I were carrying ours in case we ran into cripples.

I asked them if they had done any good. One said, "No, but if you guys care to join us we know where a small bunch of elk are - right now - and they're close to us."

Since, now, they were afoot instead of horseback and it was 4:00 o'clock I figured that the elk did have to be close by. He said, pointing toward a small stand of pines up on the mountain side, that they had seen the elk enter the stand a few minutes ago and they hadn't come out yet. He suggested that if we got on the ball the four of us could surround the timber and make a drive.

I asked him if he wasn't afraid that a game warden would hear the shooting and come up to investigate. He said, "Naah, there ain't no damned game warden up here in this storm." It was snowing a little then, but nothing like it had been up on top. As I looked back at him I could see that they weren't concerned about a game warden bothering them. I said that I'd heard that the warden from Meeker got around and that you never could be sure when or where - or how - he might show up. I added that it might be a little risky killing an elk before season opened. The hunter replied, "Ah, hell; you won't see that S.O.B. from Meeker up here this far from a nice warm pickup cab. Three days ago when we came in he was driving towards Meeker, settin' on his dead butt in a steam-heated pickup instead of out in the cold lookin' for law-breakers."

I glanced at Jack who was about to bust - and I was having trouble not doing the same. Our new "friend" then said that if we didn't want to go along and probably get our elk close by they'd better get a move on so they could get their elk and gut 'em out before dark. Also, by morning their tracks and any sign of hunting would be blotted out by the snow storm. I could feel my blood pressure rising as I stepped out of the saddle next to this fellow. When I unzipped my heavy coat so they could see the game warden's badge on my shirt I told them that I was "the S.O.B. riding around in the steam-heated pick-up". Upon hearing this news both men looked like they had just seen a ghost and turned pale. The more talkative one opened his mouth several times before any words would come out.

Taking both of their rifles I found that each had rounds in the chambers. I inspected both men's fingernails and knifeblades, but couldn't find any traces of blood or tallow on either. Checking their hunting licenses revealed that both men were from Grand Junction, Colorado. I asked them where they had gone horseback that morning, and why they had taken their rifles along if they were just looking around as they claimed. The quiet one of the two spoke up and said that while they were only scouting they didn't want to leave their rifles in camp because they were afraid someone would steal them.

Although I could have issued them each a summons for being out of camp with a rifle within the three days before season, I knew that I'd have to go to Meeker with them for a trial and this would use up two days at best. (Then there was no P.A. - Penalty Assessment - ticket; so I would have to appear in court with them.) Also, I still hoped that there would be an opportunity to apprehend the early hunters in the Marvine Peak area. This had been my first priority. In addition, I knew that the word would get around fast about the encounter I'd had with these two; so I gave them a good "chewin' out" and let them go. Of course, if they had killed an elk it would have been a different story.

The continuing adverse weather conditions thwarted my efforts to "bust up" the gang of Marvine Peak early hunters that I'd been "In Pursuit" of. From all indications they never returned another year.

Chapter Seven

When I first moved to Meeker and took up my duties as district game warden of Rio Blanco County I met the local sheriff, Bob Fulton. Bob was a few years older than I, but we hit if off right from the start. He had grown up on a resort east of Meeker, and like me he'd started hunting and trapping as soon as possible, knowing the ways of the "bush", so to speak. Bob was a big man, over six feet tall and weighed around 200 pounds. It wasn't long until we were working together, looking for cattle rustlers, game law violators or - what have you. One such instance occurred involving a fellow from out of state who had bought a ranch up White River east of Meeker. He and his family used the ranch as a summer retreat for a couple of months each year. This is the same time - from about mid-July on - that a lot of people considered that the deer and elk had fattened up and were ready to poach whenever they needed or wanted some meat.

One night as I was trying to relax after a long day of patrolling a man called me and said that he had some information on deer poaching east of Meeker. He never told me his name, nor did I ask. He said that he was returning from fishing at Peltier Lake and had heard a rifle shot. Since the shot was in the evening and in the direction he was going he had suspected some illegal hunting. As the trail he was on crossed a small clearing he approached with care. Sure enough, on one edge of the clearing he saw two men bending over an object on the ground. He said that he was almost on top of them before they noticed him. By then it was too late for them to duck into the timber. He told me that one of the men was the son of the ranch owner; the other was the fellow who ran the ranch for the owner. They had started to gut the buck they'd just shot, he said. My next move was to drive down to the sheriff's office where I found Bob, and enlisted his help for the following day.

Since these men had been caught "red-handed" according to my informant I didn't think that they would attempt to get the deer out until the next day as they would need a horse to pack it out.

Bob and I made plans for our next day's operations. We would use the sheriff's auto and drive up the public road past the ranch buildings to a point where I would jump out and Bob would continue on up for a distance, then come back showing up again at 11:30 a.m. I was going to work up high on the hillside across the valley opposite from where the deer had been killed. I would be over a quarter of a mile from the ranch buildings and in case I spotted anyone coming off the hill with a pack horse I could intercept them at the buildings. This way my pickup would not be seen in the area and alert the poachers.

A tall dead aspen had blown down over the edge of the road several days before, but it didn't obstruct traffic enough to cause anyone to remove it. If I were to leave the hillside I was on I was to tie my handkerchief on a bush under this aspen as there was a four-foot bank it hung out over.

The plan was that when Bob came back around noon if he didn't see the "flag" - my handkerchief - he was to leave and come back at about 3:30 p.m., and pick me up near this log. If nothing had happened by this time probably nothing would and we'd have to abort the deal.

At precisely 11:30 I saw Bob drive by slowly and, not seeing the white flag, he drove on up the road to a point out of sight from the ranch, turned around and drove back past the dead aspen and on down the road, out of sight.

The day dragged on without a sign of anyone at the ranch taking action that would suggest trying to get illegal meat out of the timber. By 3:30 I was ready to work down to the aspen at the road. My eyes felt like they were popping out of their sockets after looking through binoculars all day. When I got down to the aspen I sat down on it - about six feet from the very stump end of it. I didn't notice any bugs or ants at the time.

I'd been sitting there a few minutes when I heard a vehicle coming my way. I couldn't have been over twenty feet from the bank where the aspen stuck out over the road. Upon hearing the auto approaching I slid off the log and as soon as I was certain that it wasn't Bob I laid down beside the log where I was hidden by tall grass and some small brush. The auto - a pickup - pulled just past the protruding aspen - and stopped!

At first I thought perhaps I'd been seen and the driver was going to investigate. Shortly a man got out of the truck, slammed the door, and then I heard the tail gate being opened. I took a quick peek and saw the driver, a fellow I knew, lifting an axe out of the back of the pickup. I didn't want this guy to see me and instantly I knew that he was going to chop on the dead aspen; but I didn't know where he'd start. On top of this I didn't know where he would STOP his wood-cutting!

While I was trying to decide whether I should stand up and announce my presence I heard another auto coming. At this same time the wood-cutter took a hefty chop at the dead tree end sticking out over the edge of the road. This sent a shock wave up the tree trunk which I could feel as I lay against the log. About this time I heard the second car stop - and - the wood-chopper took another swing with his axe...again sending a shock up the tree.

Then I heard Bob say, "Hi, Floyd; whatcha' doin'? Looks like you're gettin' your winter's fire wood chopped up." Floyd's answer was lost due to a stinging sensation about the middle of my back - then another on my left thigh. My first thought was that the shock waves running up the log had stirred up a nest of bees. Not hearing any buzzing, though, I knew what was taking place. Floyd's chopping on the tree had stewed up some red ants which had taken up "squatters' rights" under the bark of the log - near where I lay! The next ten minutes were about all I could handle. When I'd feel an ant crawling on me I would manage to pinch him before he nailed me.

About the time I was ready to give up, walk out and try to think of an alibi I heard Floyd say, "Well, Bob, I'd better get going; I'll come back in the morning and finish chopping up this log." "O.K., Floyd; I'll see ya'." With that Bob drove off and Floyd dropped the axe in the back of his truck, slammed the tailgate shut, climbed in the cab and drove on up the road. The pickup was hardly moving when I came up off the ground like a coiled spring, slapping at the ants crawling under my clothes.

In a few minutes Bob was back and I didn't lose any time getting into his car. When I told him what had happened and what I thought of a guy who would stand around and B—-S—- while his friend was being eaten up by ants he really got a good laugh out of it, and asked me how I'd like to be called "#!**-ANT-BILL" from now on. My reply to this suggestion was unprintable.

Two years later I learned the full story on the buck shooting. The hunters quartered the animal, put it in meat sacks so the blow flies wouldn't ruin it, and hung it in a pine tree several hundred yards from where they'd killed it. They waited two days, then packed it in to the ranch after dark. This information came from a young man employed at the ranch when the incident occurred. Trouble was - it was two years too late!

But - some of Bob's and my future operations proved much more successful as will become evident.

Chapter Eight

One fall it started raining, turning to snow, a day or two before the opening of hunting season. Consequently, all travel off of the oiled or graveled roads was really sloppy going. Also, this storm triggered the beginning of the deer migration out of the high country. That would cause more road hunting than in an average year. So, it was no surprise that during my patrols I was seeing more sign of road hunting. This prompted me to do more night patrols. The complaints also started coming into the sheriff's office from ranchers who thought some of their stock were being rustled by the hunters, too.

So, Bob Fulton and I decided to team up again - this time on night patrol. That way, every time a stop was made to check out a hunter's license they would see that both branches of law enforcement were working together. We made sure that we mentioned that fact to all we contacted, hoping that the word would spread - and it did, we found.

One night we had patrolled up to the Buford area, then back to the Buford-New Castle road - and on up to the top of the mountain. We had seen quite a few deer crossing the road headed west and to the lower country. So far, though, we hadn't encountered even one car traveling either way.

About 9:00 p.m. - when we were probably half-way down the mountain - we came around a corner and here sat an auto with out-of-state license plates - and the driver was standing beside an old doe that had just been shot. After we stopped I walked up to him and asked what he was doing. Before he realized who we were he answered, "Gonna' gut the deer I just shot." He had one of the damnedest messes you ever saw!

He had just shot the doe in the middle of the road while she was standing in the light of his headlights. Then, he had cut an eight inch slit in her stomach. He would reach inside her stomach with the thumb and forefinger of his left hand, get hold of the small intestine, pull out about ten inches of it and whack it off with one slash of a butcher knife that had an eight inch blade. This was one of the best examples of how NOT to dress out a deer!

After watching this disgusting operation for a time I told him what he was in for. The charges were: killing a deer by artificial light, shooting game from a public road and - the unlawful possession of ONE FAWN DEER that he had shot earlier we discovered.

It had already been loaded in his car and it was a mess, too! Of course, he had no license for the fawn.

Needless to say, informing him of his violations didn't improve his disposition or lend any great enthusiasm to his continued gutting of the old doe. The crap really flew after he heard all of the charges. Finally, Bob told him to ease up - and showed him how to do the job right. But, Bob would not help him do it, nor would I.

After the fellow got the doe gutted and cleaned up a little we loaded it and then made him complete the job on the little fawn. I wrote him a summons on the charges and we all drove to Meeker.

The seized meat was donated to the Welfare Department, and after the trial the next morning, as we walked from the Justice of the Peace's chambers, Bob said, "You know, I would have been able to go along with almost whatever decision the Judge made, even if he let the old guy go, if it wasn't for the way he was gutting that deer!"

As the season wore on the night road hunting got progressively worse; so I would hit the off-road camps during the day, and night patrol the main roads after grabbing a bite to eat. As indicated by my diaries, and one kept by my wife for a five-year period, my hours of actually being on duty averaged eighteen hours a day. The longest continual day was twenty-seven hours and fifteen minutes.

An officer has to be in exactly the right spot at the right time and have a little luck to catch a spotlight hunter. It takes less than five minutes to shoot a deer, jump out and throw it in a vehicle, jump back in and drive off. Often they will gut it somewhere else, where there is little chance of being caught.

One night when I was working between Meeker and Buford I saw where numerous deer had crossed the road, headed for the lower country, their winter range. About 10:00 o'clock I was headed back up toward Buford when I saw several autos going rather slowly; so I assumed they were looking for deer. It was snowing lightly, but it wasn't very cold. Finally I met a car pulling a high boxed-in trailer. I made a mental note of this as I continued on up the road.

About a half a mile from where I'd met this outfit I saw a big pool of blood in the other lane. I jumped out with my flashlight and inspected the scene. It was easy to see that the deer had been loaded into a vehicle headed west - the opposite direction from what I was headed. The pool of blood was still steaming, and I had been by this spot not twenty minutes before without noticing anything of this nature.

I could plainly see that no car tracks had been made over the drag marks of where the deer had been loaded, so I could only tie it to one outfit, the auto-trailer combination that I had just met back down the road a short distance.

I jumped back in my pickup, turned it around and gunned it down the road "full bore" to overtake the car-trailer. They had gotten down the road farther than I expected but soon I saw tail lights ahead. I drove up beside the car just before going around a turn, dropped back a little and turned on my red lights, knowing that this was a little curve and I would be able to see any approaching lights.

When the driver saw the red lights flash he shoved his foot into the carburetor and took off. I could get seventy miles per out of my pickup in a very short distance; so I soon overtook them and turned my siren on. As there was no sign of the guy stopping I eased up beside the car - red lights blinking - siren wide open. Finally I crowded the car until it came to a stop. Pulling slant-wise ahead of the car, I climbed out with my flashlight and stepped up to the driver's side, a little back of the door. The driver rolled the window down and spoke. "What'sa' matter, Boss?" I could see that there were two men in the car. I told them who I was and that I had found where a deer had just been killed up the road in the last ten minutes. I continued that I had reason to believe that they had killed it and loaded it into their trailer. Then I asked them to both get out; I wanted to look in the trailer.

As we walked around to the back of the outfit I shined my light on the door and saw that it was locked with a padlock. As I ran my light on down the door I wasn't surprised to see blood dripping onto the road. "All right, open that door and let's get the deer out of there," was my next command. One of the men said, "We doan' have the key for that lock; this trailer belongs to another guy. Besides, that ain't blood ya' see runnin' out; our coffee jus' spilled when we stopped."

That was a likely story if I ever heard one, and made no sense whatsoever! I told them that if they didn't get that door open pronto I had a pinch bar in the pickup that would sure as blazes open it. That announcement prompted an immediate change of attitude and one of them said that if I'd keep my shirt on he would open the lock. He did, and stepped back. I told them to get on the other side of the trailer (so they couldn't "jump" me without needing to take a couple of steps first). Then I jerked the door open and as I did so a big four-point buck started to roll out the door. The weight had shifted just enough when they came to a stop, and the deer's head was right against the inside of the door.

Instantly the driver exclaimed, "Well! Wouldjya' looka' what's in there! Now, WHERE the hell do ya' s'pose HE came from?"

"Quit play-acting and get the deer out of there," I demanded. The buck was as limp as a dishrag, with steam coming out of his mouth and off the blood in the trailer. I told them to get their hunting licenses out, then drag the deer around into the car's lights and gut it.

When they had finished that task we loaded the deer in my pickup and then drove on into Meeker. I had the deputy sheriff register them in the "CROSS BAR HOTEL" for the night.

The next morning at 10:00 a.m. the two appeared in court. The Judge asked me for my testimony and when I'd finished he asked the hunters if they had anything to say in their own behalf.

The driver said, "Well, Mr. Judge, we been camped in the snow up on this Ripple Crick Pass. When we got in las' night we wuz jus' plain tard o' stompin' through the snow, and cookin' for arsefs; so we jus' jerked camp down and started drivin' ta' Meeker. We passed up a dozen deer; this wuz the thirteenth one we seen - wuz a buck, too; so we jus' shot 'im. Boy, we jus' got goin' good when THIS guy shows up - jus' lack "Wild Bill" in the ol' days!" His partner added, "Yeah! Thirteen shore ain't no lucky number!"

They were probably "head shy" from there on as

the fine and costs ran close to $600.00.

(Violators never received much sympathy or leniency from this one particular Justice of the Peace if he had been called away from a pool hall poker game to hold court. Especially if he was winning!)

Chapter Nine

It came to pass that the Department's policy dictated that employees must take accumulated vacation time within a certain limit or, to put it another way: USE IT OR LOSE IT.

This was the best reason I could think of for booking a Yukon hunt.

So - in the evening of a clear, beautiful, sunny day Vic Hotte, his wife, Phyllis and a horse jingler and I pitched our camp on Nichols Creek in the Yukon Territory, then hobbled and belled the horses. After chasing them upstream from camp we turned our attention to supper and a welcome campfire afterwards when there were discussions of the hunt to come.

Vic was an outfitter and guide in the Yukon, an expert on Dall sheep hunting. He wanted to check out this area for a ram he had seen several times in the past; he called him "Old Black Horns". He'd tried for this ram many times, but never could get a hunter set up right to take him. Vic thought that we just might be able to locate this trophy and, if not, perhaps we would still find a good ram in this area since he hadn't hunted it the previous fall. He had also seen a lot of grizzly sign on other trips to this location.

The next morning we saddled up and headed up a side stream of Nichols Creek, towards the mountains where Vic had last seen the ram. When we would reach a good vantage point where we could glass a lot of country we would "tie up" and check the area out with binoculars, and sometimes with the spotting scope.

During one such stop we were able to count fifty-two ewes and lambs on one mountain and three fairly good rams to our right. In the opposite direction there was a herd of thirty seven caribou with two good white-necked bulls. As we were walking to our horses, tied up in some willows, we saw a big grizzly going over a ridge about three quarters of a mile from us. This was, without a doubt, a game animal paradise as we found it that day. On the other hand, the next time a person viewed this area he might see only a small portion of this much game - or none at all.

Since I was making a 16mm promotional movie film for Vic I really wanted to get set up on that band of sheep, and also hoped to get some footage of grizzlies if possible. Vic's decision was to try to work up on the sheep as the grizzly was traveling and would no doubt be hard to catch up with. Also, the three rams we had seen just might work over to the ewes, too. The balance of the day was spent trying to get movies of the sheep. The only chance we had was down-wind and the sheep spooked, clearing out on us. From here we headed back for camp.

It had been a beautiful fall day in the north country and although we had no footage of game, nor had we found "Old Black Horns" I still felt it was a day well spent. We had seen a lot of wildlife and several places where a grizzly had made sizeable excavations in a hillside to get a gopher. It's amazing the amount of dirt and rock a grizzly will dig out to capture a half-pound rodent! On the way back to camp we kicked up several coveys of ptarmigan. The way they would peel down over a hillside with an occasional wind behind them would really make excellent pass shooting with the old Model 12 scatter gun.

As mile after mile of this wonderful, uncluttered, unspoiled country passed under our saddle horses' hoofs I couldn't think of a more peaceful situation.

Back in camp after a hearty supper we made plans for the following day. Vic decided that we would head into the area north of camp, and especially to one particular mountain where he had seen "Black Horns" once.

Next morning when we left camp it was all fogged in and ready to rain. As we topped out of the Nichols Creek valley it started to drizzle. About mid-morning we decided to "hole up" and wait for the "soup" to clear up around the mountain we wanted to hunt. After considerable effort we got a willow fire going and dried our gloves - and toasted our sandwiches at noon.

About 1:30 when we were about to give up, the

clouds started lifting around the mountain tops and the drizzle let up. Vic looked around and said, "Let's get those old broom tails and head for the top; maybe by the time we get up there all that soup will be moved out."

About an hour later we tied our horses just below the top of the mountain. On top - like so many high spots in the Yukon - it was fairly flat. Some six hundred yards from where we topped out we spotted five sheep. When the fog cleared out completely so we could get a good look at the sheep we saw that all were rams - two small ones and the other three were good heads. Sure enough, one of the rams was "Old Black Horns"!

The two small rams were near an outcropping of rock which was our only route to stalk the three big ones. We bellied up until one of the small rams spotted us and, although not spooked, yet he was certainly curious. The wind was in our faces so he couldn't smell us; but if he spooked - no doubt he and the other small ram would run towards the three big rams - and surely spook them.

When we first saw the sheep I noticed that the ram with the very dark horns was broomed heavily - more like a bighorn, while the other two had about 38-inch curls with perfect points. Vic whispered to me, "Bill, we've gotta' do something quick or those little rascals are going to stampede and upset everything; so - where do you want to shoot from?" I guessed the distance from a rock ahead of us about the size of a water bucket would be around 275 yards. If we could reach that rock without blowing the deal I could use the rock as a rest. With the ram standing broadside - and with no cross wind - this shot would be a piece of cake for my 7mm Mag.

We eased forward on our bellies with our chins down touching the grass until we reached the rock. Vic stayed behind me to run the movie camera while I made the shot. By this time all five rams were alert and about to take off. I eased the Magnum up over the rock, using my gloves as padding. As the cross hairs settled just back of "Old Black Horns" shoulder I applied pressure to the trigger. At the flat-sounding report of the Magnum "Old Blackie" didn't fold up like I had expected; but bolted for about twenty yards, stopped, and broadside again - looked our way. The nearest young ram that was about 80 yards in front of and below the line of fire must have thought the world caved in with the blast of the 7mm as he took off full-tilt for the rim.

I slammed a new round into the chamber, lined up with the scope on the ram and dropped the hammer. Again - nothing connected with the ram! This shot headed the sheep out of the basin and I let 'em go, not shooting again as I KNEW something was wrong with my scope.

Vic stepped up beside me and said, "What the hell's wrong with your shootin'? That ram was standing broadside on both shots." Right then I didn't KNOW for sure WHAT was wrong; but I was convinced of one thing: my scope was off.

This mountain top, as most of them in this area, was thickly covered with six-inch grass and the ground was very damp. Due to these conditions it was impossible to see where my two shots had hit. I couldn't tell whether they were high, low or off to one side. We checked the spot where the ram was when I shot but couldn't find any hair, blood - or, even where the bullets had hit. It's no sin to miss a shot now and then; but it sure shakes up your confidence to miss two broadside standing shots like I had!

After this episode we got our horses and headed off the mountain's rim, leading the horses as it was pretty steep getting off this old hill. The only brush or trees on the mountain were along a small stream that rushed down to the flats below. Our descending course would intercept this line of willows close to the bottom. Upon nearing the willows, which were about fifty yards wide, I suddenly saw a grizzly stand up in them - around 125 yards from us.

Just as I said, "Grizzly!" to Vic the bear dropped out of sight. He had heard us no doubt and also saw us when he reared up on his hind legs; but he hadn't gotten our wind as the air current was blowing uphill.

I snaked the Magnum out of the saddle scabbard just as the bear stood up again, at a different place, and a little closer to us. Each time he stood up so he could see over the six-foot high willows I'd have to swing to a new spot and before I could line up and shoot he would drop down. On about the fifth time he stood up he was about eighty yards from us and the horses were getting nervous. Perhaps the action of the horses caused the grizzly to hesitate a little longer than the previous times which enabled me to line up the scope on his Adam's apple and squeeze the trigger. As the 7mm recoiled I heard a solid "thunk" and the grizzly vanished as if by magic. After the sound of the shot died away it was so quiet it hurt your ears for a few seconds. As I watched, one certain willow top jerked a few times near where the bear was when I shot. I said to Vic, "Well, there's our grizzly, Pal." He replied in a concerned tone, "Oh, hell yes! After missin' a ram twice what makes you think you got the grizzly with one shot?" I mentioned the tall willow stick jerking after I shot, and the way the grizzly dropped - I was sure he was down.

We waited about five minutes and didn't see or hear anything from the willows. It was decided after throwing several rocks into the willows, with no response from the grizzly's quarters, that Vic would take the horses across the little stream at a narrow point of the willows, well above where the grizzly had been, and watch for any action from him.

Meanwhile, I would ease into the willows and try to locate the bear. I must confess right here that this action will make the hackles on the back of your neck stand up when you can't see ten feet ahead of you and you aren't absolutely sure what condition the bear is in. I soon came to the little stream which left a brushless winding course about eight feet wide along it. I started to ease downhill along this route as it was the only place where I could see any distance and also get off a shot if necessary. As I stepped around the brush at a bend in the stream's course I suddenly saw the grizzly - about twelve feet from me. Needless to say, this sudden encounter with a grizzly really snaps you to attention. The grizzly was stone-dead and lying at the base of a high willow stick, the one I'd seen jerk earlier.

We dragged the bear out into the open and upon examination found that the bullet had hit dead-center of the brisket, going through and breaking the spinal column, causing instant death. The bullet had struck about six or seven inches below the line of sight. This was pretty good proof that my gun was shooting much too low, and apparently caused me to under-shoot the ram.

After taking some pictures we skinned the bear and headed for camp, arriving before dark. The following day we tried the Mag. at a hundred yard target and were astounded to find that the impact of the bullets was twenty-one inches low at that yardage. We both fired three shots at the target and each time the shots landed in the same spot in an area about the size of your hand. (Later it was disclosed to me that one of the help, when packing items into the main camp, had knocked my gun off of the rack it was on, and had said nothing...)

I've often wondered if I'd known that the rifle was shooting this much off when we bumped into the grizzly what decision I'd have made about shooting at him. I'm sure, though, that I probably would have tried anyway.

In Whitehorse, at the Yukon Game Department headquarters the officials used one of the bear's small teeth to check his age and came up with thirty-one years. (They split the tooth and then count the "year rings", similar to the method used to age a tree.)

Even though I failed to collect "Old Black Horns" I wound up with a good ram later on during the hunt. The stalk, the shot and all worked out very well for the movie. In another week I would be back in Colorado, on duty as a game warden again.

Chapter Ten

One fall a few days after hunting season opened Bill Roland, the game warden for the Craig area, contacted me in Meeker just before noon. After the usual comparing of notes we decided to have lunch at one of the local cafes and continue our talk.

We entered the cafe and dropped into a booth next to a couple of other men who were wearing their hats. We noticed that the hats had red covers stretched over the crowns; no doubt these fellows were hunters. At first we didn't pay any attention to their conversation until I heard one of them mention "Park Creek". The only Park Creek I knew of in the Rio Blanco County area is up the South Fork of White River. That creek flows into South Fork.

I signaled Bill to listen and see if he could hear what these guys had to say about "Park Creek". One of them said that he had killed a cow elk in the upper end of the big park that the creek flows through. He said that they wouldn't be packing any meat out to the South Fork campground for two or three days; they wanted to get an idea of where the game warden was working so there wouldn't be any chance of being apprehended.

Bill and I were dressed in Levis, light colored shirts, and wearing regular western hats; so there was no giveaway as to our professions. We tried to gain more information while we ate our sandwiches, but we couldn't make out any more on the elk kill. We did learn that they were camped down in the South Fork Canyon on the opposite side of the river from the trail that runs up the canyon to the high country.

After paying our tab Bill and I went out and sat on a bench across the street from the cafe so we could watch for the two hunters to come out. I wanted to see what vehicle they got into and what the license plate was. In about ten minutes they came out, walked up the street and got into a four-wheel drive pickup with Colorado plates. I told Bill I'd probably be checking on these guys soon.

After Bill left I started getting gear ready to make the trip to my cabin on South Fork. From what I'd gathered from comments by those two hunters it seemed that they would no doubt be camped at a cabin about three quarters of a mile above mine.

The following day I hauled my saddle horse and pack horse up to some private property a mile short of the South Fork campground and left my State pick-up and trailer there. From that point I had to ride on up through the campground and then up to my cabin near the mouth of Lost Solar Creek.

There were a lot of vehicles and horse trailers parked in the campground and as I rode through I located the pickup that the two hunters got into the day before in Meeker. Therefore, I figured that they would be camped up South Fork.

It was a little after noon when I arrived at the cabin; so I decided to wait until the morning to start looking for the hunters. Then, on second thought, toward evening I saddled up and made a scouting trip past the cabin that I expected those hunters to be using. The cabin is across the river from the trail so I rode on past it for a half mile or so until I could get up on a point above the canyon bottom where I could see their cabin and some of the trail leading to the Park Creek trail. In the flat by the cabin three horses were grazing; no smoke was coming from the chimney. Naturally, however, I wasn't able to see into the pine trees back of the cabin. I waited until about 5:00 o'clock and then rode back to my place. I'd get ready for the searching trip tomorrow.

I was up at four bells the next morning and after breakfast I saddled up my two horses and headed up Lost Solar Creek shortly after daylight. Since I didn't have to lead my pack horse I made good time. It was all uphill until I reached the top of the Lost Solar trail. From there I rode on east to the head of the Park Creek trail, then down to the upper end of the big meadow where I figured the cow elk had been killed - the one the hunters had mentioned in the cafe.

I got up high enough that I could see most of the upper end of the big park, unsaddled the horses and put Sally on a picket rope so she could graze. My pack horse, Kit, would stay with Sally without being picketed. Then I made myself comfortable against a big aspen tree, ate my lunch and — watched for magpies with my binoculars.

(After an animal has been gutted it isn't long until the magpies find the site. Usually if the birds fly into a place and in a few minutes fly back out it indicates that they have found something to feed on. If you're wondering the reason for this practice, it's because when magpies find a kill they'll often tear off a piece of the meat and fly to another location to eat it - alone - and away from the "crowd".)

About 2:00 o'clock I saw two maggies fly into the edge of the aspens across the park from me. I watched for about five minutes and then another maggie flew into the same place. It no sooner went out of sight than one came boiling back out with something in its bill and flew into an old dead quakie. By now I was almost sure I'd found a kill site.

I checked the horses to see that they were all right, then edging into the timber I walked over to where the magpies were flying from. Sure enough - I found where two elk, a cow and a calf, had been gutted and their heads cut off. I was pretty sure that the calf belonged to the cow since the cow's bag had milk in it and was lying close to the bigger gut pile. I couldn't find any carcasses, however. Apparently they had been packed out as was evident from the sign of horse tracks made on top of the blood-soaked ground.

I saddled my horses, then followed some horse tracks from the site of the kill to the Park Creek trail where the tracks turned down towards the South Fork. It was close to 5:00 p.m. by the time I reached the cabin where the hunters were staying. There was smoke coming out of the stove pipe now and several other horses were hobbled out in the flat. As I stepped off my horse one of the hobbled horses whinnied at my horses. I quickly tied Sally to a convenient post, turned and started toward the cabin. As I did so the door opened and a man stepped out and spoke. I greeted him and as I was walking toward him I noticed that at the corner of the cabin there was a hind quarter of an elk sticking out from underneath a piece of canvas. At this point a woman poked her head out the door, and, upon seeing me, jerked back inside pronto. Although the fellow could see the badge on my jacket he asked, "What can I do for you?"

I told him who I was and asked him how many were in the party. He said that there were five men and the woman, the wife of one of the hunters. When asked, he said that they were hunting elk.

By this time the other four men had come out of the cabin. I checked their licenses and then asked where the lady's license was, if she was hunting also. I saw the one man shoot a quick look to another and then answered, "I guess she has it." I said that I wanted that license, too; so he went to the cabin and got the license from the woman.

Walking over to the corner of the cabin where the small hind quarter was hanging I noticed that some of the meat had been cut off, probably that day. Also, there was a carcass tag on the meat that corresponded with the number on the woman's license. One of the fellows said that she had killed it and they were using it for their meat supply. I asked them if they had gotten any other elk and if so where they were. The spokesman for the group said that they had gotten two OTHER BULLS and that they were hanging on the meat pole out in the pines back of the cabin. I still had their licenses in my hand and had noticed that the carcass tags had been torn off. Then I said, "Let's walk out and see the other elk." There were two bulls there all right - on the meat pole, tagged and unskinned. I thought to myself, "Well, they won THIS round, but I wonder who'll win the NEXT one?" I asked them which of them had killed the calf that was being used for camp meat.

During all of this exchange I recognized one of the men who had been in the cafe two days ago; he wasn't saying much. One of the fellows spoke up and said, "The lady shot the calf; by mistake." And, since they didn't want it to just lie out there they brought it into camp. At this point I thought it would be worth trying to shame them into telling the truth. The lady had a bull elk license and the meat was this year's bull calf; this much I knew from looking at the pelvic bone. At this stage of the game it was considered "an antlerless elk", and I was quite sure in my own mind that one of the men had actually killed the calf.

I said, "The guy who shot this elk had better tell me because none of you have an antlerless license and, if none of you shot it then the lady would have to be the one who did, as you've said. But, I don't think any of you would be small enough to throw the blame on her." No one spoke up; so I told them that I would give them just one minute for someone to admit to killing the calf, or I was going to summons all of them into court for illegal possession of an antlerless elk, and if they thought I was bluffing to call me on it.

In just a few seconds one of the men spoke up and said, "I shot the damned calf - because I didn't think we had near enough meat to last us until we were through hunting."

I summoned the man into court for illegally killing an elk and for the unlawful possession of an elk. He was fined $250.00 and costs. So - I won THAT round.

(Earlier, though, back at the cabin, when I'd questioned them about the COW elk, none of them - supposedly - knew anything about her. Without a "corpus delicti" I couldn't pursue the matter further. Later, however, a renegade I knew told me that he had packed the cow down to the campground and hid it in the willows for these guys.)

Chapter Eleven

"Are you the Game Warden?" a voice at the other end of the line asked. "Well, yes, I'm A game warden," was my reply. "Listen, you don't know me so you won't know who told you this - but I've got some information that you should have. Don't ask any questions; I'll tell you what the deal is; then it will be up to you to do something about it." When the party on the other end of the line finished I thanked him, with my assurance that I would get right on it.

The information was regarding a situation involving elk poaching east of Buford during the present open season. At the time of receiving this call the season was about two-thirds over. According to the informant there were two hunters camped up high under the Flat Tops. He said that he had hunted several days in the same area and had talked to one of the hunters quite a few times. These hunters were from the east and would be pulling out the following night around 11:00 p.m. so they would reach Meeker sometime after midnight. Also, he was sure that they would have more than their legal limit of two elk. He had seen two calves hung up in a pine tree close to their camp, and he felt that they could have been taken only by these two guys. Further, he warned me that these men had bragged to him that if any blankety-blank game warden bothered them they would "smoke" him up, pronto!

The caller was quite definite about the two hunters being tough, and advised me to be prepared for trouble. I reassured him that I'd use caution, but I would need a description of their outfit. He readily complied.

Now I was armed with the valuable information I needed about their vehicles. I knew the makes, the color and even their license numbers. So, the following day I alerted the other Game and Fish personnel in surrounding areas; they would now be on the lookout, too. Then I contacted the local Town Marshall, Sam Cron, to see if I could enlist his help since my plan could well include his presence. Meanwhile, I sent information to the check stations in both Rifle and Idaho Springs, Colorado. That about covered everything - except...

...My Back!...So I contacted a good friend, my hunting partner Keith Dunbar. I was certain that I could depend on him and that he would "cover" me in case I needed him. I would handle any trouble I could SEE, but sometimes your "Blind side" is exposed to the enemy.

Fortunately, Keith agreed. And, Sam would cooperate, too. Now, everything was ready for the "Reception Party"!...

The logical route for these hunters would be to follow the White River road down to Highway 789, then through Meeker, if they planned to go over Loveland Pass (there was no Eisenhower Tunnel then). Or, they COULD turn right at 789 and head to Craig, going on over Rabbit Ears and Berthoud Passes into Denver. Regardless, I wanted to be ready to intercept them either way they might go.

There's a stop sign at the junction of the river road and 789, and I would have bet that these hunters were not going to make a stop at that sign, especially so late at night.

At 11:30 we were all positioned. The plan was to have them stopped initially, if possible, for a traffic violation (for not stopping at the stop sign). That way it would take the pressure off of the "tipster". If I was to stop them right off the bat for any suspected game violation I feared that my informant might get hassled, especially since these guys were supposed to be tough.

Around 12:30 we saw car lights lighting up the sky around the bend from the stop sign. In just a little while the lights came into sight and, without hardly slowing down, the vehicle — towing another outfit - ran through the stop sign and turned left toward Meeker. Falling in behind I was asked where I wanted them stopped. "Get 'em under a street light so I'll have 'shootin' light' if necessary."

The Marshall stopped them under the second street light coming into town, and jumped out - and down the driver's throat for running a stop sign. At the same time I went around to the right side of the outfit and ordered the man on that side to get out.

When the fellow got out of the car I told him to step around into the light, and asked him and the driver both if they had been hunting. They looked at each other and hesitated; so I told them I wanted to check their hunting licenses. Without saying a thing, they dug out their licenses. Both had bull elk licenses. Bulls Only.

When I asked them if they'd had any luck one of them said, "No, we haven't done any good - and - we HAVE to be back to work — RIGHT AWAY!" Well, I sincerely doubted part of that reply, because I could see blood soaked into his trousers on one leg. And, they were nervous. As I watched their faces, and noting where my counterparts were, I said, "Well, Gents, I want to see just what you have in these outfits." The response was, "If you tear anything up you'll have to pay for it!"

By now I was sure they had illegal game. I climbed up into the pickup and moved a box out of my way, then reached in under the tarp covering the load. The first thing my hand met was the front leg of a calf elk. I turned my flashlight under the tarp and saw that there were several quarters, all stacked under the tarp.

I hopped out and told everyone what I'd found and said that I wanted the hunters to drive to the back of the courthouse where I would shake the outfit down (in more light).

When we'd finished looking the load over we had found three calves and one cow elk, in quarters. This made four illegal elk. (Oh, I might mention that by now these guys were very docile. Didn't seem that

they were ready to"smoke" me up, pronto - or whenever.)

I seized the Jeep pickup, the four elk and all items
connected with the violations. Summonses were
issued to appear in court the next day at 10:00 a.m.,
after they'd spent the night in jail.

These men were found guilty of illegal possession
of four elk and illegally hunting elk without a valid
license.

Their fine was in excess of $2,000.00.

(Rumor has it that the next fall these same hunters
were picked up for illegally hunting antelope.)

Old habits die hard.

Chapter Twelve

My district included Trappers Lake, headwaters of the White River. The lake attracted lots of fishermen, so - needless to say - I checked hundreds of anglers fishing these waters. Sometimes I would spend up to four or five days in this area. The Department had a cabin on the lake and it was headquarters for the game warden as well as for the personnel who took the native trout spawn. Back in the '30's the spawn gathered here would be taken to a hatchery located down where the parking lot is now. Of course, the building is gone at this time, with the spawn being taken to a hatchery elsewhere.

I'd been up in this area for a couple of days, checking the fishermen at Little Trappers, Surprise and Wall Lakes. Now it was time to start checking Trappers.

Soon after I'd started my "rounds" I met a lady walking up the trail with four or five trout on a stringer. As I introduced myself I said that I was checking licenses and asked her for hers. While she was digging out the license I thought I'd try to strike up a conversation with her to relieve whatever tension my appearance might have caused. "That really is a nice pole you have there, Lady," I commented. (It was, indeed. Bamboo, and very sharp-looking.) At my remark, however, she came UN-glued, and in short order she set ME straight on the subject of a "pole". "Young man," she replied, "this is a ROD - NOT a 'pole'! Anything that costs $75.00 and over is a ROD. UNDER $75.00 - now THAT is a 'pole'; DO you understand?"

After THAT blast I sure as hell DID understand - and never wanted to make THAT mistake again! It was in record time that I copied her name, license information and the number of fish she had, then headed on around the lake muttering something to myself about "fisherwomen!" and $75.00 fishing "rods" - or "poles" - or willow sticks - or what-the-hell-ever...

About an hour later I'd worked around the lake to an area that had rather shallow water out into the lake for perhaps a hundred yards or so. Quite a ways out there was a woman in waders who was fly fishing, and she was doing a beautiful job of casting the fly. I stopped to watch her for a few minutes and, since I didn't have rubber boots on, I didn't want to wade out to her to check her license. Instead, I shouted to her, "Mam, I'm Bill Goosman, the game warden from Meeker, and I'm trying to check on the fishing here at the lake; would you please give me your name, address, license number and tell me how many fish you have?"

"WHO did you say you are?" she asked. I repeated, "I'm Bill Goosman, the Meeker game warden." After a few seconds she declared, "You CAN'T be! I hear that Goosman is old, very tall, homely as hell and meaner than cat sh...er...ah...I mean... Oh...ah...meaner than...uh.....all-get-out!" With this announcement she waded to shore and took a really good look at me. By now we had attracted quite an audience. People had heard the loud talking and were gathering to see what it was all about.

One fellow, hearing the exchange - but, obviously not the CONTENT, drew a wrong conclusion and really "bore down" on me. He squinted up his eyes, glared at me and said, "It looks to me like if you wanted to check this lady's license you should have had to wade out to HER, rather than demanding that she slosh to shore so you could stay dry." I gave the guy a go-to-hell look, grumbled under my breath some unintelligible comment relating to his ancestry and then got the heck outa' there. It was hardly worth the effort to try to straighten out his misconceptions of the whole event.

The rest of the day went more smoothly and after completing my duties here at the lake I decided that it was time to "take a hike" - up to the high basin where I was quite sure there would be no fishermen - or fisherwomen...only chipmunks, snowshoe rabbits and - perhaps - some elk to watch.

I didn't know it then, but there was to be an incident later on at Trappers Lake which would test my mettle to a somewhat greater degree.

Chapter Thirteen

Although the Game and Fish Department had progressed a long way in every respect from back in 1937, it still lacked some in catching up with the times. For instance, the game wardens were issued autos or pickups depending on the type of district involved. Usually the mountain districts dictated pickups while the eastern slope with its flat country was more adapted to sedans. But, the pickups were two-wheel drive, while the hunters and fishermen were equipping themselves with jeeps and other four-wheel drive outfits that put them 'way out ahead of us.

(In those days most mountain wardens carried a chuck box with food needing no refrigeration, bare essential cooking utensils, a plate and some "tools".

Even so, many of my meals consisted of candy bars, and my sleeping quarters were often on the pickup seat.)

After World War II most of the auto industry started turning out pickup trucks with 4-wheel drive. We game wardens who used pickups were soon issued the new 4-wheel drive units to replace the former 2-wheel drives. This fact was a huge step in keeping up with the hunters and fishermen. In addition to the 4-wheel drives we were being provided with two-way radios. The two-ways really bridged a great gap in our operations and cut down thousands of miles per year that we would have had to driven to accomplish the same communications which now only took minutes by radio.

One day at about 8:00 a.m. when I was a few miles west of Meeker my thoughts and the steady purr of the pickup engine were interrupted by the radio call, "Car Three-Two-Five, Meeker, Car Three-Two-Five." (Car 325 was my call number.) I picked up the mike and answered, "Meeker, Car 325, go ahead."

"Car 325, you are wanted at the Marvine Ranch as soon as possible. What is your 10-20 now?" I gave my location as approximately six miles west of Meeker. "Car 325, on your way through Meeker the sheriff suggests that you pick up your lariat rope." My question, "What am I to do with my lariat, help brand calves up there?" (Sometimes on my days off, if lucky enough to have a day off, I'd help a rancher brand calves if he needed an extra hand.) The answer was, "You will find out when you get there!"

Marvine Ranch is located on Marvine Creek approximately thirty-eight miles east of Meeker. "Car 325, can you accept this request right away?" "10-4, Meeker; I'm on my way now!"

On my way through Meeker I stopped at my home and threw in my "lass" rope. Try as I would I couldn't figure why I'd need my lasso - and not my saddle!

When I pulled up before the buildings at the Marvine Ranch and stepped out of my pickup I was met by John Dole, the foreman; with him was his young son and one other man who was employed at the ranch. After the usual greetings I asked John with a grin, "Who do you want hanged around here, John?"

"A blankety-blank black bear!" he retorted.

Right after breakfast John and the rest of the ranch people were startled by the squealing and ruckus at the barn. Their immediate investigation revealed a large black bear trying to fish a half-grown pig out from under the barn where the pig was lodged - and the bear couldn't quite get a grip on the pig. He could scratch the terrified pig across the rump, but he couldn't get a toe-hold on the porker!

All hands at the ranch knew that the owner of the ranch, a millionaire who loved wild animals of all kinds, would not permit even a chipmunk to be harmed as long as it was on his property. They knew that he would not allow the bear to be shot unless some human life was at stake. (His ranch was bordered by National Forest; so, most of the year there were either deer, elk, a bear or two and other critters ambling about on the ranch.)

John and the others had used rocks, clubs, a car horn, and an old wash tub for noise trying to run the bear away from its intended pork dinner. When I asked John where the bear was now he said, pointing toward some big pines, "Up there - in one of those trees, and he's madder'n a hornet, too!"

"What are you going to do with him, Bill? Mr. Barbour is over at the lodge and he said for me to get you and have you take the bear away, but not to hurt him. Do you think you can rope him?" I answered the question with, "Well, perhaps; but what the hell do you suggest I do with him after I rope him?" John wasn't quite sure, but maybe he could think of something.

I knew that I had to do something - to try to get rid of the bear without shooting him - unless he attacked a person. I reached in the pickup and brought out my .357 Magnum and slipped the holster onto my belt. I knew by now that THIS "Teddy-Bear" wasn't afraid of people and that if I harassed him much - which I'd have to do - things could get sticky.

I swung the cylinder out on my six-gun, checked to see that all chambers were loaded, then dropped it back into the holster. I reached in the back of the pickup and grabbed my lariat rope; then I asked if someone could show me the bear. John's son was really getting all fired up by now about the "catch-'em-alive and-drag-'em-out plan". He said, "Sure, Bill; I can show 'im to ya'," and started toward the trees. I stopped him and told him to take it easy and, by all means, not to get ahead of me — just in case the bear decided he'd had enough roughing up already.

Before we could see him we could hear him - popping his jaws. That is plenty of warning that the bear is hot under the collar and about to commit mayhem if pushed any farther. Easing up behind a bush I could see the bear standing at the base of a pine tree. There was no doubt that this bear was not to be fooled with any more without him coming unglued. I certainly wasn't foolish enough to step up THERE and try to rope him!

I motioned to the boy to follow me and we'd back out of that "powder keg" before it blew up and somebody - including the two of US - got peeled up.

A plan was forming in my mind; a way to trap him IF I could find the material necessary to make a "catch-'em-alive" trap. Then, too, maybe - just maybe - the damned bear would take off before I could build a trap!

I explained my intentions to the men watching the situation and John said that he would try to round up whatever materials I needed.

"I need a 55-gallon drum with one end open - or at least one that we can cut the end out of. Then, something to make a trap door, and 50 to 75 feet of rope to act as the drop rope for the trap door. Also - I'll need something for bait."

John thought for a minute, then sent the hired man off to empty an open-ended barrel used to store oats for the horses. Next, he asked me if I thought some fried chicken backs and wings would do as bait. Since this was Sunday and his wife was going to have chicken for dinner there'd probably be left-over backs and wings - not the most popular pieces of the chicken. So, why not feed them to the bear?

He sent his boy to the house to order the bear's menu from the cook. Then he went to the saddle shed and came back in no time with a hundred feet of quarter inch rope. When he motioned me to follow him we walked to the shop and leaning up against the shop was the answer for a trap door: a screw-type headgate with frame that would just fit the 55-gallon drum's open end.

We started to put the trap together and in about thirty minutes we had it ready. We packed the con-

traption up to about thirty feet from the brush and
pine trees where the bear was. I had hoped he would
be gone, but no such luck! Apparently this was the
same bear that had been raiding the Marvine Creek
campground about a mile above the ranch. This
would account for his boldness around people.

NOW! The trap was set - baited with fried chick-
en! The heavy door was raised, held up by the quar-
ter-inch rope running back to where I was (out of the
way, but where I could see if and when the bear
entered the trap). If the bear cooperated and went
into the trap, I'd turn loose of the rope letting the
door slam down - and the bear would be trapped!

We no sooner got organized than the bear came
around the brush, picked up the first chicken wing
bait and then proceeded along the baited trail to the
drum trap. I thought to myself, "When you go in that
barrel, Buster, I gotcha' - with your rump to the trap
door and you can't turn around in that drum!"

Well, the old bruin wouldn't go in the trap! He'd
look in and sniff real loud, reach a paw in as far as
possible, but he couldn't reach the bait at the far end
of the barrel. He wouldn't go in for the fried chicken
in the drum!

When I was sure that he wasn't going in the trap I
threw a club at him and dropped the heavy trap lid at
the same time hoping that this would run him off.
Instead of taking off he ran up to the pines and
climbed up in one tree about twenty feet. When he'd
reached a suitable crotch he settled down in it like a
1934 sod-buster taking up squatter's rights on the
plains.

Our next try at getting rid of Mr. Bear was to turn
the garden hose on him. Since this was July and

quite hot, the cold water was most welcome to him. He'd face into the hose stream and lap up all the water he could.

By this time a number of people had heard about the fracas with the bear and were starting to show up. Some offered their advice; of course, none of them volunteered to put their ideas into motion.

Well, I was the local (or - loco?) game warden and supposed to be able to handle any given situation involving wildlife; so I'd better do something soon. At this point I got the crazy idea of climbing the pine tree next to the one the bear was in and - ROPING him!

Among the people arriving to see (and bet on) who would win out - the bear or me - was Bob Hilkey, a resort owner and horse-shoer. Bob was a good hand with a rope, and said that he would help if I'd tell him what to do.

I told him I'd climb the tree next to the one the bear was in and try to rope him. If I could, we'd jerk the bear out of his tree and then I wanted Bob to rope one of the bear's hind feet. If we could do this we could cram the bear into the drum and I'd haul him off.

As I climbed the tree with the lariat rope looped over my shoulder the bear kept an evil eye on me and growled a few times. I reached a level with him and started trying to cast my loop over the bear's head. On the third try the loop settled over his head. He immediately reached up with one front paw and took a swipe at the rope. Instead of knocking the rope off - he rammed his paw and leg through the loop! At this point I jerked up the slack and the wreck was on! The loop was now around his neck and back of one front leg.

Any adult bear is a powerful animal and this one would weigh around 275 pounds - and he was getting madder by the second. I soon saw that I couldn't hold the bear because I needed one hand to hold onto the tree. I threw my end of the rope down and hollered at Bob and two other guys to try and grab the rope and not let the bear climb any higher in his tree. Also - if he tried to get over in MY tree to jerk him out and I'd be right down to help them. Bob came back with, "What the hell do you want US to do with him if we jerk him out? I'm not up to wrestling a wild, mad bear!"

(First off, I didn't really think that they would jerk the bear out of the tree; so I told Bob that the bear would fight the rope long enough for him to take a dally around a cedar post which would keep the bear off of them.) Then, if they would keep taking up slack we could finally get another rope on him.

To be honest about it, I certainly wasn't sure what would happen if and when the bear hit the ground. If he bit the rope in two he was just as apt to take on Bob and any other people nearby as to make a run for it. One thing I did know for sure and that was: I'd shoved all of my chips into the center pile and now I'd better play my cards right or I might find myself trying to blast this critter off of someone with my .357 Mag. Frankly, right then I wished that that pistola was one of those containing endless cartridges like used by the cowboys in those Wild West movies I'd seen.

I started down my tree as fast as possible, dropping from limb to limb and as I reached the last limb some eight feet off the ground I heard some snapping sounds up in the bear's tree. As I started to swing down to the ground I saw Bob and his helpers give a hard jerk on the bear's rope. As I hit the ground and fell sideways the dislodged bear hit the ground about fifteen feet from me. The bear recovered much quicker than I did. As I had told Bob he would, the bear started fighting the rope, turning flip-flops, bawling and slapping at bushes or anything in his way. I yelled at Bob to get a dally around the cedar post, which he did. He later said that it was the fastest dally he'd ever taken.

I jumped up and grabbed Bob's rope which was lying coiled up near me. I used to do quite a bit of heel roping when helping brand, and was quite good at it. I knew that this would be the most important heel roping I'd ever do; it was absolutely vital that I get a rope on a hind foot of the bear so we could stretch him out. Sooner or later he was going to bite the other rope in two and nobody knew what would happen then.

I shook a loop in record time, then ran up to the rear of the bear and made my cast. Luck was certainly with me that day as I caught the left hind foot on the first try. Another good husky guy that I'd never seen before ran over and grabbed onto the rope with me and, with Bob and his two guys holding a tight dally around the cedar post we were able to stretch the bear out

"Somebody get that trap over here!" I bawled at the pop-eyed crowd.

By now the bear was slowing down as his wind was being squeezed off by the first rope which he had managed to get looped around himself in such a way that he was choked down. When John and two others got to the trap they pulled it up to where I wanted it and then we pulled the bear up to the mouth of the trap. If he hadn't been so choked down it would have been a heck of a job to get him into that trap.

After getting him in the drum we closed the lid down two-thirds of the way, and wired it. Then, after getting our own wind back, we finally took the ropes off. My rope was chewed up pretty badly, but I was thankful that it was just the rope instead of some human that got chewed up (including yours truly).

We loaded trap and bear in my pickup, then parked in the shade so the bear could cool down. We sprayed him as much as possible with cold water - then let the water run over the barrel to cool it and him down.

John's wife, Opal, had kept Sunday dinner warm, and when we had the bear secured we were invited in to eat. (I don't recall that there were any wings or backs!) We learned that over thirty people had shown up for the "BLACK BEAR RODEO".

After dinner I drove up to Blair Mountain - with four carloads of observers following. I turned the bear loose — no worse for the wear - except for his pride.

As far as we knew that bear never bothered Marvine Ranch or the campground again.

A number of those witnessing this event are still in the Meeker area. Unfortunately, my roping partner and good friend, Bob Hilkey, is no longer with us. But he used to ask me every so often if I'd like to rope a bear again.

My answer was always colorful!

Chapter Fourteen

As I finished the last bite of hot cakes topped with thick maple syrup the phone rang. After I said "Hello", a voice on the other end replied with, "Hi, William: how busy are you today?" Immediately I knew that it was my district supervisor and that he had something important on his mind. Almost 100 percent of the time when he started out with this type of a greeting to me over the phone I knew that I was going to drop whatever plans I had had in mind for the day and would wind up working on some other assignment. Usually it would be something more important than what I had lined up to do.

When I answered that it was nothing that couldn't wait awhile he asked me to meet him and another warden at his home in an hour.

As I pulled up in his driveway I saw another Game and Fish pickup parked there also. The unit belonged to a warden from a district considerable distance from White River.

Inside, I greeted Cleve and the other warden. After some small talk Cleve said that there was a problem over in this warden's district, "and it needs immediate attention." Cleve continued, "It's unusual, and - it COULD be dangerous; the man involved has a history of erratic behavior, to say the least."

This fellow owned a ranch and put up around two hundred tons of alfalfa hay. He was a cattleman and, of course, fed the hay to his cattle. This was during the years when the mule deer population was at its highest. Naturally, when the snow got deep, covering a lot of the deer's feed, and the temperature dropped down from 10 to 35 below zero the deer flocked into the ranch lands and did considerable damage to haystacks. Any stacks that weren't fenced with deer-proof yards usually got a working over by the buckskin.

This warden had been in his district for years and he knew most all of the residents. He had a lot of friends and, of course, via the "Grape Vine" he kept track of what was going on in his area.

According to the information he had gathered the rancher in question was supposed to be trapping deer with steel traps set around his haystacks. The rumor was that when he caught any deer in the traps he would shoot them with a .22, throw them on the hayrack and cover them with hay. Later he would dump them in a brushy area where the coyotes, eagles, magpies, ravens, etc. would handle the situation from there.

Although exceedingly cruel, this was a very effective procedure to eliminate some of the deer from feeding on his haystacks. He had boasted about this maneuver, and when asked whether he should cover the traps so they wouldn't be found by a game warden, his reply was to the effect that any man had the legal right to trap jack rabbits, and if by some vague chance a deer was found in one of his traps it was caught "accidentally" and, of course, would be released. As to any blood found on the snow around the haystacks, that also would be attributed to the killing of jack rabbits. In those days a jack rabbit was considered in a class with rodents, causing a lot of damage to ranch lands, and so it was a legal target whenever you found one.

The plan to apprehend this man who was applying such a harsh and painful method of deer-control was developed by four of us: Cleve, the warden from the district involved, Bill Roland, the Craig warden, and myself. The culprit had been encouraged time after time to use deer and elk fencing which the Game and Fish Department supplied; but he wouldn't have anything to do with it. Therefore, it seemed best that the supervisor and that district's warden work in the background.

The next day the three of us, Cleve, Bill and I, traveled to the town closest to the "action" and settled in at a motel. That evening Bill and I were to "scout" the area. This rancher was reported to be a tough guy and it was said that he would "come apart" if caught by the law and taken to trial. In fact, a number of people around the area had said that he would start shooting the minute a game warden caught him, if given a chance. As a consequence, we were to proceed with all caution.

Bill and I were dropped off at the side road that led from the highway up to this rancher's hay fields and haystacks. We were quite sure that the rancher wouldn't show up until the following morning when it was time to feed his cattle and check the traps.

As the Boss and the other warden drove away Bill and I hurried out of sight of the road; we weren't to be picked up until after dark. The "snow road" led us up onto a mesa where the rancher's fields and haystacks were located.

We checked a hay yard containing a full stack and a half-used one being fed off of. There we found two double spring traps set around the stack; but nothing else.

From here we followed sled tracks to another yard with three stacks in it. The sign around it showed that quite a few deer were coming in and feeding on those stacks. We were careful to stay on packed snow so we didn't leave any "man" tracks around the stacks.

Our inspection of this hay yard revealed four #14 Newhouse double spring traps set around the yard, and one Keflock snare which was tied to a big seven-foot cedar post leaned up against the end of one stack. The snare hung down in an inverted "vee" created by the cedar post and the end of the haystack. It was set to hang about thirty inches high. It was quite obvious to us that it wasn't intended to catch a rabbit - even a high hopping one! The only other critter that it could possibly be used for would be a deer.

Naturally, we didn't bother anything but we certainly made mental notes of where each trap was set.

From here we followed a hard-packed deer trail across the field to where it crossed a deep irrigation ditch some three or four feet wide. At this point we followed up the ditch to where we were hidden from the stack yards by oak and serviceberry brush. This point would make an ideal location to check out the area with binoculars tomorrow morning.

By this time the January daylight was fast turning to dusk; so we headed off the hill to meet our ride down on the main road.

After we'd had supper and were back at the motel we went over the details of circumstances as we had found them that p.m. Again - Bill and I were informed that we would be dealing with a very unstable man in the morning, provided that we caught him molesting deer.

The next morning we all ate an early breakfast and shortly before daylight Bill and I were dropped off where we'd been picked up the evening before. About thirty minutes later we were positioned in the irrigation ditch at the point we had chosen for our surveillance.

At the stack yard where the rancher had been doing his feeding we could see an old doe lying down, out some distance from the edge of the stack. We were probably a quarter mile from this stack yard and even with good binocs we couldn't determine whether she was in a trap or just lying there resting after feeding for most of the night.

At the other yard, nearer to us where the snare was set, it was a different situation. We could plainly see that the cedar post at the end of the stack had been knocked down and moved away from the stack some distance. After studying the scene a few minutes through our binoculars we were able to make out the form of a deer lying close to the snare post.

Without a doubt the rancher's snare had caught a deer during the night!

Now - all we had to do was wait - until the rancher came up to feed and check his traps.

By the time we'd sized up the situation concerning the traps and snare we were about froze out. Both of us did a considerable amount of body-slapping and foot-stompin' to drive out the cold. We learned later that it was 14 degrees below zero when we left town that morning.

We had about decided on our method of operation when a team of horses pulling a hayrack appeared up over the rim at the far end of the field - headed towards the first stack yard. As the rancher's outfit came into view of the old doe lying down she turned her head and looked his way, then she jumped up and made a lunge towards the fence. In doing so she was pulled off her feet and jerked backwards as she came to the end of the apparent trap chain. The rancher very calmly climbed down off the hayrack with a rifle in one hand and walked over to the lunging deer. We saw him stop, raise the rifle and fire at the doe.

"He shot that old doe with a .22!" exclaimed Bill. (From the report of the rifle we both knew that it was a small caliber gun.)

The doe made two or three more attempts to get away, then fell down. When she fell the rancher socked his rifle down, butt-first, in the snow so it would stand up and keep the action clear of the snow. Then he jumped on the deer (we assumed to release her from the trap). We continued to watch his activities and all of a sudden he stood up and kicked at the deer. She also jumped up, cleared the yard fence and ran across the field on a deer trail, disappearing into the brush that bordered the field.

"Well! What do you make of THAT operation?" Bill inquired. I replied with, "Looks to me like the old boy is living up to his reputation for dirty tricks - gut-shootin' and releasing the deer he catches. We'll try to find out before this deal is over."

The rancher retrieved his rifle and made a circle of the one and a half stacks in this yard, then walked out to the rack and climbed on. He headed in our direction to the stacks where the snared deer was.

We had already decided to follow the deep irrigation ditch down to the closest distance from that stack yard - then climb out when he was behind a stack and hope that we could get to the yard before he saw us. We each had a high-powered rifle and also a six-shooter in a shoulder holster.

Needless to say, we were "keyed up", not knowing what the rancher would do when he saw us. We had spread out with about thirty yards between us so it would be more confusing for the guy to watch both of us at the same time.

When we were about fifty yards from the stack yard the rancher walked into sight on the far side of the yard and leaned his rifle up against the fence, then walked behind the stack again. By this time we had almost reached the yard. Now the rancher came around the end of the stack that was closest to me. He was so intent on checking his traps that he didn't even look up. As he knelt down and picked up an unsprung trap I looked at Bill; when Bill looked at me I quietly patted my rifle and pointed to the rancher's rifle. Bill nodded his head in reply that he understood my silent message. I wanted one of us to have control of the rancher's rifle.

Bill set his rifle down by one of the fence posts and as he started to cross the fence I said in a fairly loud voice so the rancher would turn directly toward me, "Good morning!!" At this interruption of an absolutely dead quiet the startled old boy almost jumped up on the end of the stack. I heard the loud clang of the double spring Newhouse trap as it snapped shut when he dropped it. He straightened up and looked right at me, then noticed Bill who had stopped about half-way across the yard and just a few feet from the dead deer in the snare. It was a 2-point buck.

"Where the HELL did you two come from - and WHAT are you doing up here?" exclaimed the rancher. Neither of us answered directly, instead I asked him if he had seen anyone else up here the day before. He said, "No, I haven't seen anyone else up here all winter. Now what do you guys want?" By this time I had stepped over the fence and now stood a few feet from the man.

I told him who we were and that we wanted to talk to him about the deer trapping. His face at first was about the color of putty, then it turned red. Without saying anything he started toward the fence where he had left his rifle. Bill was already on his way to the rifle and since he was much closer to it than the rancher was I knew Bill would take care of the matter.

I said to the rancher, "Hold it, Mister - forget the gun! You are outnumbered and you know it!" This seemed to snap the guy back to reality. Bill picked up the man's gun and pumped the live round out of the chamber, then pulled the magazine tube out and poured the rest of the .22 bullets out, leaving the gun completely empty.

Between the two of us Bill and I explained to the rancher what he was up against and advised him of his rights. At this point the rancher spoke up and said, "Well, you seem like nice young men trying to do your jobs. If you want me to, I'll haul that dead deer off the hill for you." We thanked the old boy, but declined his offer. At the same time, though, we were completely flabbergasted at his meek demeanor!

We confiscated his rifle, six #14 Newhouse traps, the snare and, of course, the 2-point buck. The rancher continued his cattle feeding chores while Bill and I dragged the buck off the mesa to the highway where Cleve and the other warden picked us up.

The rancher was summoned into court and given a sizeable fine. From this point on he accepted game fencing for his haystacks. He was watched pretty closely from there on, but gave us no more trouble.

Chapter Fifteen

I buckled my safety belt as the pilot taxied the heavily loaded Beaver float plane out onto Watson Lake in the Yukon Territory. Our destination was to be Frank Cooke's base camp at Scoop Lake in British Columbia.

As we gained altitude, circling back over the lake and the scattered town, also named Watson Lake, my mind raced ahead to the up-coming stone sheep hunt which I was about to embark on.

Soon we passed the boundary between the Yukon Territory and British Columbia, headed for stone sheep country. The flight to the base camp was smooth and pleasant which enabled me to enjoy the magnificent scenery.

Upon landing we met Frank Cooke at the dock.

From here we went to have supper and hold a pow-wow. The plan was that I would continue to the famous Colt Lake the next day where I would meet two other hunters, the guides, cooks and other camp help.

The next morning my gear as well as other supplies were loaded into a float-equipped Super Cub with Terry Cooke as pilot, and we headed for Colt Lake. Terry did a big share of the flying for Frank and is a top-notch bush pilot.

We passed over Colt Lake and the camp, then banked around to make the approach for landing. Making this approach and the landing was kinda like driving a Jeep down a big rock studded wash back home! With such a narrow approach lane and a cross wind the pilot had to be looking right down the sights to make everything work.

A lot of sheep hunters have hunted out of this camp, and over the years some excellent rams have been taken in this area. Colt Lake got its name years ago when well-known Skook Davidson was guiding hunters in the vicinity. One time Davidson and his party camped over night at the lake. The next morning when the horse jingler rounded up the horses it was discovered that a white colt had been foaled during the night. Skook named the lake "Colt Lake" in honor of the new addition to his horse herd.

The balance of this first day was spent sighting in rifles, shoeing horses and getting supplies packed in preparation for the trip into a fly camp, one that Frankie Cooke called "Buck Brush".

All I planned to take on this hunt was a ram, if possible, and - a lot of film for a promotional movie concerning Cooke's outfitting and guiding business.

After getting settled in at the fly camp the first day out we spotted a herd of eighteen ewes and small rams at about 10:00 a.m I shot some footage of these, then we continued on in quest of larger rams.

Shortly after lunch one of the guides saw a ram on the skyline about a mile from us. As we watched, five rams crossed over the skyline and joined four more rams, making a total of nine. We set up a couple of scopes and found that two of the rams were in the 38-inch class. Since we hadn't split up yet to work separate routes back to camp it was convenient to have a herd of rams headed our way. The other two hunters there could make a try for the two good heads in the herd. I'd be photographing.

A route for the stalk was quickly planned, hopefully enabling us to intercept the rams on our end of the mountain for which they were headed. I left my rifle with the horses and took only my 16 mm movie. I'd try to get footage of the stalk - and the shooting, if we lucked out. The little ravine we were following fizzled out sooner than we'd expected so when we got to the head of it we eased our heads up and were surprised to find that the rams had traveled faster than expected. They had already arrived at a point where two or three big boulders stuck up just under the sky line. One of the big rams had apparently gone over the skyline with a couple of the smaller ones. The other big ram was standing on one of the boulders which was about the size of an auto.

Frankie sized up the situation and said, "There's your ram, boys; if anyone can make a 400-yard shot." One of the hunters named Fred who was hunting with a .300 Weatherby said, "I think I can do it," and pushed his down jacket ahead of him on a rock to rest his rifle over.

I have done a lot of shooting and consider myself a good judge of distance, and agreed with Frankie that the distance was a good strong four hundred yards - uphill also. I was sure that Fred would shoot, but didn't expect very good results.

At this point the ram turned broadside, walked to the left edge of the boulder and looked over the side at something below him. I had hastily set up so as to get the hunter and the ram in the movie view finder. I'd no sooner pushed the release on the camera when the British Columbia stillness was shattered by the blast of Fred's .300! To my surprise the ram did a flip flop off the boulder and rolled a short distance down the hill. Needless to say, Fred was congratulated for the excellent shot he had made. Upon reaching his ram the tape was applied to the horns and found that the head measured slightly over thirty-eight inches!

I spent three more days working out of this camp, but didn't find much to photograph after Fred collected his ram; so Frankie and I returned to Colt Lake. For about a week we hunted out of the Colt Lake camp in all directions. All we could find were ewes and small rams. I burned up quite a bit of film on sheep during this time.

Often in the evenings at camp, or when taking a lunch break, Frankie would mention an old ram in the area, one that had a broken right horn about half way up while on the left hand side he had a tremendous horn that Frankie and others judged to go forty-two or forty-three inches.

One morning as we headed into the area where old "Broken Horn" hung out I told Frankie I'd settle for Old Broken Horn if we could find him.

By noon we had only seen a few ewes and no

rams of any size. After eating lunch we sat around using the glasses to search the area for any possible sheep. A good two miles from us we spotted a lone sheep, high on a mountain, just under a saddle. Since it was in the direction we were heading we mounted up and worked our way up the valley towards the mountain the sheep was on.

A half hour later we came to a point where the valley forked three ways. As this looked like a good place to glass a lot of the area we rode in behind a thick stand of pine about eight feet tall. We dismounted and dropped the reins - since most of Cooke's horses were broke to stand "ground-hitched" - unless left for a long period of time. Even then they would just go far enough to graze.

Frankie pointed towards a big rock about the size of a bushel basket and said, "Let's set up the spotting scope on that rock and see what we can find." I grabbed the scope and left my rifle on the saddle since we'd be close to the horses.

Soon after I was comfortable I spotted a ram bedded down on a small shale slide, a good half mile away. In short order we spotted nine rams lying around on the slide. Frankie started checking them over with the scope and suddenly said, "I'll be darned! There's 'Old Broken Horn', laying right under the middle of the saddle!" I soon crowded to the scope so I could take a look at "Old Broken Horn". Since his left side was toward us I could get a good look at the unbroken horn and it was a dandy! Two more of the rams had good heads in the thirty-seven to thirty-eight inch class. We immediately started searching the mountain for a route to stalk the rams.

Frankie turned around to look behind us and immediately froze. He said, "Don't make any quick moves; there is a bunch of sheep looking right at us a couple hundred yards away!" I turned around slowly so I could see the sheep. There were twelve head of small rams. After deciding that there wasn't a good ram in the bunch I turned back to looking for a route up to the nine head of rams bedded down on the shale slide.

Just as I started looking through the glasses Frankie said, "Easy! Here come some rams." I turned my head slowly and looked in the direction he was looking and there coming around the point that divided two of the forks of the valley, and about 375 yards away, were seven rams. A quick look through the binoculars revealed that all of the rams were from thirty-five to about thirty-nine inches.

We were really caught in an embarrassing situation! We were sitting around the rock like a couple of old fogies having tea while my rifle was a good sixty feet away - in the scabbard on my saddle! The sheep were traveling so we had to act immediately, but in a way so as not to spook the rams.

Frankie said, "Let's try to look as much like a moose as possible by walking one behind the other. When we go by the horses we'll get your rifle and head for the end of that stand of trees."

When we got to the horses we were hidden from the sheep by the trees. I slid my rifle out of the scabbard and joined Frankie at the end of the trees. We were trying to determine which ram was the best and find a way to get an open shot other than off hand at that distance. All of a sudden the rams stopped and threw their heads up, looking in our direction. At the

same time, out of the corner of my eye, I saw movement behind and to the side of us. Of all times! The
blankety-blank horses decided to walk out into the
flat where there was some good grass to graze on! In
a low voice those two saddle horses were called a lot
of names and none of them were flattering. Right
then I had the urge to make bear bait out of both of
them!

I glanced back at the rams and saw that they were
starting to move out. Frankie said for me to take the
dark one in the middle of the herd, and slightly down
the hill. The point that the sheep were on was covered with flat rocks - some about as big as table tops -
and most were lying parallel with the sloping hillside.

There was no chance to pick a place to shoot from;
so I did the next best thing and slipped the 7mm
Magnum up alongside a small pine. This wasn't too
steady; but it helped a little. I tried to squeeze off the
shot as the cross hairs wavered across the ram's
shoulder. As the Mag. recoiled I saw the 150 grain
Nosler bullet kick up a cloud of rock dust from one of
those sloping flat rocks - barely over the ram's shoulder!

The rams really took off as that shot echoed across
the mountains. Frankie said, "You broke the left front
leg." This statement surprised me as I knew my shot
was slightly high.

As I slammed the bolt home on a new round I
realized what had happened. The bullet had struck
the flat-sloping rock and ricocheted upward under
one of the rams directly above the dark one that I'd
shot at. In so doing it broke the ram's leg. By now
the crippled ram was mixed in with the others and a

follow up shot was impossible for fear of hitting the wrong ram.

We watched the sheep climb higher on the mountain. Just before they went out of sight the crippled ram pulled off to the left and lay down. This was the break I was hoping for. I stepped up on my horse, leaving Frankie to watch the ram and to direct me to him in case he worked on up the mountain before I could get into shooting range. I swung far out to the right and while still on horseback, climbed up on the mountain until I figured that I was on a level with the ram.

As I dismounted I checked Frankie with the glasses. When he saw that I was looking at him he motioned that the ram was still where he had lain down. I worked around the side of the mountain to within about 150 yards of him when he jumped up and took off like a turpentined cat. A snap, off-hand shot sent the ram rolling with a broken neck.

When Frankie climbed up to where I was he viewed the sheep and produced a steel tape to give the head a rough measure. We found that the right horn measured 38 1/8, while the left one went 38 4/8.

"Well, Bill, from now on a fella had better tie up his damned horse before getting mixed up with ram shooting," commented Frankie as he started to cape the ram. I agreed - and began taking pictures.

Although he was far from making the record book he was a good representative of the species and one of twenty-eight rams we could see at one time.

When I looked up toward "Broken Horn" the group he was in was standing bunched up on the skyline. I waved him farewell and turned back to my camera.

Chapter Sixteen

For the first two or three years after moving to Meeker it sounded like a small war going on up on the Flat Tops a day or two before season opened. I decided to slow this down and my boss was in favor of doing just that, too. So, I made plans to join the dudes who were waging war against wildlife.

Hauling my horses up to the Marvine campground I parked my pickup and trailer in some thick pines as best I could and then rode forth toward the Flat Tops. On my ride I heard close to a dozen shots and most of them sounded like they came from the area where I was headed.

I camped on top that night, on the edge of a small park where I could picket my horses on good feed.

Right after sundown I heard three shots east of where I was. And, certainly, it sounded like the second shot had found its mark due to the "thud" right after the shot. In the morning I would sure check that area out.

The next morning - two days before season opened (officially) - I rode out of the timber into the edge of another small park that was about a hundred yards across. On the far side I saw two horses tied up; they were saddled up with pack saddles. As I started across to the pack horses one of them whinnied at my horses. Immediately a man stepped out of the timber, apparently to see what the ruckus was all about. Then, another man appeared.

The fellows just stood there until I reached them. I spoke to them and remarked about the weather, then asked them if they needed some help. One of them said, "It looks like you may need some help yourself - to load something, since you have an empty pack horse." (I'd left my camp back at the place where I'd pitched it the night before.)

As I stepped down off my horse I asked them where they were camped and one of them said, "Over near the trail going down Bear Creek." This was a little south of where we were.

I could see that both men had blood on their hands as well as dried blood on their clothes. As I looked past them into the trees I could see the exposed part of an elk lying on the ground. "Who killed the elk?" I asked. One of them replied, "We aren't sure; we were both shooting at it."

My next comment was, "You guys haven't gutted many elk, have you? Then, "Are you hunting on your own or are you with an outfitter?" The answer was, "Naw, we don't need a guide - and - what makes you think we haven't dressed out many elk?"

By this time we were close to the elk, and I could see that it had been turned to lie over night with its stomach down. Of course, it was stiff as a board and the men had just started to cut its head off. I told them the reason I knew they hadn't had much to do with cleaning an elk was the amount of blood splatters they had on them and the fact that they hadn't opened up the neck. They hadn't removed the wind pipe and the gullet either. In addition, instead of turning the elk with its open stomach area UP so the animal heat could escape, they'd turned the elk with the stomach DOWN which would trap the heat.

One of the hunters said, "Well, who are YOU that you think you know so much about it? If you're a butcher maybe you can help us!" I assured them that I could and would. Then I told them who I was and that I'd heard the second shot yesterday evening hit an animal. I gave them summonses for illegally killing an elk and since I only had one pack horse - and a camp to move out - I'd file only the one charge on them if they would pack the animal down to the South Fork campground (which was closer) on opening day of season. I told them that I'd meet them there about 1:30 in the afternoon.

I tied a seizure tag on the carcass and kept the spike's head as evidence. Since I had their hunting licenses - and they were Colorado residents - I figured they would show up alright.

I then helped them split the bull down the back and we loaded half on each of their pack horses. They said that they had saddle horses back at camp; so they would have a means of transportation.

I knew that the word would get out fast that a game warden was on the Flat Tops so I spent the rest of the day checking the area and the hunters. I didn't apprehend any more violators, but I did wise up a number of hunters to the fact that things were going to change up here on top.

The men arrived at the South Fork campground as scheduled. From there they went to court and were fined $100.00 each plus costs. It didn't take long for the story to get out, however, and from then on I would hit the Flat Tops at different times so no one knew just when I'd show up.

Chapter Seventeen

For years after I came to Meeker the Department made a winter elk trend count in an effort to get a reasonable census of the elk herd in the various districts having an elk population. White River was one of those districts. Usually this count was made in February, right after a snowfall, if possible.

One evening the phone rang and when I answered I heard, "Bill, this is Gil (Hunter) and I'll be in Meeker tomorrow night as we are going to fly the White River elk trend. Will you be available to fly with Kenny (Milyard), as counter?" They were going to start the day after tomorrow.

To answer his question I told him that I'd have to bow out this time as I already had an appointment with a rancher that a.m. The rancher had suffered considerable elk damage to haystacks in Stewart Gulch, a tributary to Piceance Creek. It was certainly very important to both the rancher - and the Department - that I meet with the man and work out some agreement on the damage. I felt that I had gained the confidence of the ranchers in my district, and so was determined to retain that trust if I could.

Gil then asked if I knew anyone who could fly with Kenny on the count. My reply was, "How about Butch Lauridson, down at Little Hills? I'll be down there tomorrow morning and will ask him. I can let you know tomorrow as soon as you get into town. If he can't I'll find someone else to do it." This plan was fine with Gil and so after shootin' the bull for a while I hung up.

By noon the next day I had contacted Butch and he agreed to fly the count for me. Butch was a real nice guy and easy to work with. He was in charge of the Little Hills Experiment Station located in the Piceance Creek area.

That evening Kenny came in with the Department plane for the count the next day. I met Gil and Kenny at the motel that evening after supper. We had an enjoyable time together and discussed various matters concerning deer and elk, etc. One item that came up - I'll NEVER forget! What would I do in case I was ever in a plane crash "way back in", while on a count IF I was lucky enough to survive?

As mentioned earlier, during my hitch in World War II I was, by choice, in the Air Corps, and was stationed in the South Pacific as a crew member on a Catalina flying boat in the Air-Sea Rescue Service. During my stay in New Guinea with the Fifth Fighter

Command I worked my way up from Observer to Gunner to Gunner Pilot. I was also in charge of the survival gear; so I learned a lot about self-survival, as well as survival in general, during those years of service. I saw a lot of things happen that I would never have believed did happen if I hadn't been there to see these occurrences with my own eyes.

Anyway, Kenny knew that I'd had this experience when he asked the question. I said that the first thing I'd do is be sure to have a supply of <u>stick</u> matches on my person and a common tallow candle stub, even if it was only an inch long. To my way of thinking this is the surest fire-starter you can carry. Next to having appropriate clothing a MUST when flying snow country would be a pair or two of "bear paw" snowshoes. The reason I mentioned the "bear paw" style is due to storing them in less space in the plane, especially small planes like Piper Cubs, etc.

Candy, raisins and nuts are all good for quick energy. Also, I prefer tea for a stimulating drink over all others. It's easy to make and tea bags don't take up much room.

I said that if I was forced down in the back country, and was still able to get around the first thing I would do is find a tree, a dead pine would be best, and fire it. The smoke would give a location by day and the actual fire or flames would pinpoint your location by night. Plus, the fire would keep you warm. Barring extreme bad weather there would be a search plane up in a few hours after you didn't meet your E.T.A. I told him that if he couldn't find a dead pine, then to pile up all the wood he could find and fire it using green limbs after the fire got going. That would give off as much smoke as possible.

The next morning I met the rancher on Piceance Creek, checked the damage out and headed back for Meeker. This was before the Game Department started using helicopters. About half-way to Meeker I received a call on the car radio to report to the sheriff's office upon my arrival in Meeker. The request was urgent.

At the sheriff's office I found Gil and the sheriff looking very serious - and going over a map of the Miller Creek area east of Meeker. I asked them why the serious looks and Gil said, "Bill, the plane hasn't come in yet and the 'boys' are overdue three hours now." He said that they had checked the airports at Craig and Rifle and he was afraid that they were "down" someplace.

When asked where I thought they might be I had Gil show me the flight plan as best he could. The areas they were to fly were Oak Ridge, Main Miller Creek - East, Middle and West Miller Creeks. Since I had flown this count in those areas several times in the past years I figured they were down in the West Miller Creek area somewhere.

On flights I had made in the West Miller Creek area I had experienced quite a bit of down draft, and the plane would be flying low while counting elk.

When no sign of the plane, or word, had come in by 3:00 p.m. there was no doubt in anyone's mind that the plane was sure enough down. Gil put in a call for another pilot who had done a lot of trend count flying for the Department. He wanted him to come into Meeker immediately. Since this pilot was an excellent bush pilot and knew the area very well we all felt that he could locate the downed plane.

The sheriff called in a snow cat from the

Kremmling area and by dark quite a bit of the area mentioned had been given a quick going-over. But - no sign of the downed plane.

One thing that really bothered me was the fact that no smoke or fires had been seen by any of the search parties. I was flying with one of the local pilots and really was on the lookout for signs of a fire. All of the Meeker-White River area has timber of some kind, and if a person was able to get around they could get to timber very easily and start a big fire.

The following morning the search planes were up at the crack of dawn, sweeping the area. The sheriff and I were standing by in Meeker with a snow cat to go in on the ground if the plane was found.

About 8:30 we received a call from Norm, pilot of one of the search planes. Norm said that he had just spotted something shiny in a deep cut running down into West Miller Creek. He wasn't sure what it was and the timber was so thick that he couldn't see anything else but just this shiny spot - about the size of a wash pan. He said that he would take another pass at it from the creek up and try to get a better look..."Stand By!"

A couple of minutes passed, with everybody in the office holding their breaths; then the radio crackled to life again with Norm's voice. "Meeker, I have flown over the spot again, but can't see any better, nor can I see any life around the area." He said that he did see a track coming out of the timber and cutting around the hill into some more timber. He couldn't make it out for sure, but thought it probably was an elk track. "Anyway, I'll keep looking." He gave us the location of the "shiny spot" and went off the air.

Immediately the sheriff advised all search units that we were on our way to investigate the "shiny spot", and to keep in touch.

In the group going up with the snow cat was a fellow who was good on snowshoes; he would accompany me up to the site of the shiny spot. We wouldn't be able to get up to that location with the snow cat; therefore the need of someone going in on snowshoes.

My partner and I left the snow cat and the others in the bottom of West Miller and then worked our way up another draw north of the one we really wanted to look in. Near the top of the mountain we climbed out onto the ridge separating the two ravines. Then we started working our way down the ravine, staying up out of the actual timber, but able to see all of it. While traveling this ridge we didn't need our snowshoes since the wind had blown most of the snow off.

I kept looking for man tracks crossing the ridge, but a small herd of elk had worked the area the night before; so if there were any human tracks on one of the game trails the elk had wiped them out.

About half-way down the ridge I saw a single stem of bitter brush standing on end with the bottom end up and leaning slightly against some brush. The second I saw this I knew that it had been jerked up within the last couple of days as the little hair roots were still in tact with about three inches of the main tap root.

I called attention to this and the fellow with me gave it a casual look, then commented, "So - you've found a stick with some fuzz on it, but how do you suppose this has anything to do with the airplane?" I didn't reply right then, as I had just seen what appeared to be a "scrape" several feet from the "stick". It was on the rocky ground that had been swept clear of snow.

Now, a game warden should be able to read "sign" - but try as I did I couldn't quite tie the scraped spot on the ground in with the bitter brush stem that had been turned upside down. It seemed, however, that whatever caused the scrape on the ground had also uprooted the brush stem.

We moved a few yards on down the ridge, and suddenly I saw a small piece of aluminum about the size of a playing card. Instantly I knew that we were about to see the plane wreck.

A few steps further and there was part of a wing, sheared off when it hit a big pine. Then - there was the tangled mess of the wrecked plane. I could see that someone was still in it.

"I wonder if both of them are still in it," I said. "Let's get down there and see!" "Well, Bill, you go on down and look; I'll wait up here for you." I answered, "O.K., if that's the way you feel."

I walked and slid down to the plane and found that Butch was still in it; but there was no sign of Kenny. Perhaps he had been thrown out on impact as the engine was lying up in some brush a good hundred feet from the wreckage. I immediately checked the seat belt on the pilot's side and found that it had NOT been broken; rather, it had been unfastened instead, which meant that Kenny had gotten himself out alive. Now - where WAS he?

My immediate fear was that in shock he had gotten out and wandered off into the trees and might not have survived through the night since no one had seen any sign of fire or smoke yesterday evening or this morning. And, the temperature was around twelve below last night. It then dawned on me that the seat belt on Butch's side wasn't broken, but it was undone. I knew after viewing Butch that someone else had to have undone it. Now, where the blazes could that Kenny have gone?

"Come on down; we've got some lookin' around to do," I hollered up to the fellow waiting on the hill. While he was getting down to the wreckage I was looking for tracks to see which way Kenny had left the scene. I soon found a track or two; but they were half smoothed out. I couldn't figure this deal out. It made me think of the saying: "that guy is so tired his butt is dragging his tracks out"...But, this situation was FAR from funny!

I soon made out that Kenny had left the plane and headed on a horizontal level around the ridge, towards White River. It was decided that we would go on down to the snow cat and fill the sheriff in on what we had found; then I'd come back up to try and find Kenny.

When we got back down to the group waiting at the snow cat the sheriff informed us that Kenny had worked his way down West Miller by following elk trails to an old doctor's summer cabin. Fortunately, the doctor was wintering at the cabin - for the first time in about twenty years!

Dr. Wear saw Kenny stumbling down the creek on the crusted snow early that morning, and had taken him in. Kenny had done what he thought he could for Butch, then had the presence of mind to get a down-filled sleeping bag out of the plane and headed out for civilization. He had survived the cold by crawling into his sleeping bag when night overtook him.

Kenny had a broken arm, lots of hide knocked off and was still in shock. "Doc" had patched him up, then WALKED - or WADED through the deep snow to the nearest phone on the river. He called the sheriff's office and reported the circumstances to the dispatcher. He would then return to his cabin and take care of Kenny until somebody came for him. (And, Dr. Wear had only the most limited eyesight!)

After absorbing this GOOD news our attention was turned toward the very sad task of getting Butch's body off the mountain. An old cow-puncher had shown up on the scene where the snow cat was parked and "allowed as how" we might need a good "hoss" to bring Butch out. His offer was most welcome.

Next, the coroner arrived; then the other snow-shoer, the cowboy and his horse, and I headed up the mountain. Kenny was brought to the Meeker hospital, and Butch was returned, too.

One day when Kenny had healed up and was back on the job I happened to meet him in Denver. Of course, the tragic accident came up. He told me all that he could remember about it. According to him a down-draft caught them, flipped the plane over and the next thing - all hell broke loose. When the ripping, tearing, smashing tangled mess came to a stop at the bottom of the ravine it took Kenny a few minutes to get his wits together. Of course, he immediately checked on Butch. In his dazed condition he wasn't sure whether Butch was dead or alive. Then, he found that one of his own arms was badly broken. He did what little he could about the situation, then dug the down-filled sleeping bag from the wreckage and headed out for help. Of course, he was in deep shock and acted on impulse as much as anything. He dragged the bag most of the time thereby wiping out most of his tracks.

I asked him why he didn't set a pine on fire so we could have found him the evening before. He said that he remembered me telling that and said that he considered it. But, on second thought, he was afraid that if he did so the fire might get away from him and burn everything up. He thought that there might be some chance that Butch would survive. Unfortunately, it was all over for Butch by the time the plane came to rest.

How often I have thought of that incident, and the circumstances that occurred to keep me from flying that fateful trend count!

Chapter Eighteen

One spring the snow melted out in the high country much earlier and faster than usual; so it followed that the people who ran the Trappers Lake concession were ready to take out fishermen before they ordinarily did.

To assist them they had a young man named Chuck who would run the horse hire. I knew him; we'd met on various other occasions. He would be guiding fishermen into the lakes in the area.

It was this particular spring when I decided to ride up and check Wall Lake. I told Chuck of my plans and he said that he sure would like to go along. He had a young horse he was breaking and thought it would be a good workout for the colt. That was okay with me.

When we left the horse corral Chuck took the lead - which meant that he would cross the outlet first, ahead of me. And - Chuck was SO proud of his new Stetson! He'd bought it just a few days before. It was black, naturally; his hats were ALWAYS black. It was a dandy - one of Stetson's finest.

When we rode up to the water's edge Chuck let out a wild "YAAA-HOOOO!!", spurred his colt - and roared forth into the water. It was considerably deeper than he'd expected!

The colt surfaced - with Chuck still in the saddle. But - his new Stetson was floating merrily down the stream...

Finally, emerging back on my side of the water, I asked him if he would repeat his performance. "Sorry, Chuck, but I didn't get that on film!"

In reply he told me where I could go and find a place that's hot and dry.

The trip to Wall Lake went off without any more hitches although Chuck was really down in the mouth about losing his hat. I felt sorry for the poor guy, too, in spite of my kidding.

Then, it was back to Trappers.

For years the Game and Fish laws prohibited the fishing of the inlets and the outlet to Trappers Lake during the spawning season. This was done to protect the spawning native trout. It eliminated most of the wading through the spawn beds done by the fishermen, where disturbing the beds would crush countless eggs. Some, however, just couldn't pass up the chance to try for a "spawner" in the shallow water.

Since most fish that were actually spawning wouldn't hit a fly or lure the violator would resort to the snagging procedure to hook a fish. A real "snagger" would take a large treble hook and weight it with lead. It would be thrown beyond a spawner, then dragged back until close to the fish at which time it was given a hard jerk, quite often snagging the fish in the side.

One day while eating lunch at the Game and Fish cabin located at the north inlet of the lake I saw a row boat with four people in it. It was swinging into the bank near a posted inlet across the lake from the cabin. Assuming what the occupants of the boat were up to I grabbed my binoculars and trained them on the boat.

After the four got out of the boat and tied it to some willows along the bank they started fishing in the posted spawning area. In fact, one man could have spit on a sign; he was that close to it.

I immediately terminated my lunch, buckled on my .357 Magnum, slipped my summons book into a hip pocket, slung the binoculars over my shoulder and hot-footed it down to the lake. There my Game and Fish boat was tied; it had a 7 H.P. kicker.

Just before getting in the boat I took one more look across at the spawning area. Their boat was still tied up, but the fishermen were gone. Upon not seeing anyone I was sure that they had gone upstream of the inlet which was also posted for some distance. As I pulled away from the bank I headed down the lake to about even with the concession cabin - then across the lake, finally turning toward where their boat was tied. Tying my boat, I then high-tailed it to the inlet stream.

About a hundred yards up the noisy, rushing little creek I saw all four of the fishermen, fairly close together, really concentrating on the art of fish-snagging. One of them was a young boy, about twelve years old. He was carrying a burlap sack which was used to put the snagged trout in.

I climbed up a little knoll to my right to get a better view of the operation but when I stepped clear of the brush and trees on the knoll the fishermen were gone. I looked on upstream and didn't see them; then down towards the lake where I saw one of the men step into a small opening at the lake, close to a hundred yards from their boat.

Immediately I took a short cut to intercept them near their boat. As I came out on the trail leading around the water's edge the boy was close to me. One man was in the boat by then and the other two were untying it. The boy turned around and saw me approaching. He hollered, "Hey, Dad! Here's some guy walking up!"

One of the men on the bank was a big, burley guy with a "bull neck"; now HE was carrying the burlap sack with the fish flopping around inside it. He asked me, "Where the hell did YOU come from?" I informed him as to who I was, and that I had observed their activities from both across the lake with binoculars and also up the stream. The other guy still on shore said, "Well, what's wrong with fishing these waters anyway?" I told him in no uncertain terms what was wrong with it. I continued that I also wanted to check their fishing licenses. Then I informed them that I was going to summons them into court for fishing in a posted spawning bed and especially with snag hooks.

When I told them this the guy with the big neck took two or three steps towards me, stopped with his shoulders hunched forward and asked me where they would be summoned to. I told them it would be to Meeker and that they would be taken before the J. P. soon after we arrived.

Upon being so informed he got red in the face and shifted his weight, asking me if I thought I could "take them in". He continued, "I think you'd look good thrown in the lake with the rest of the poor damned fish," and took another step towards me. The other guy on shore was stepping back up behind "Bull Neck" in an apparent move to assist in whatever action the big guy undertook.

Luckily I'd grabbed a light hip-length jacket out of the boat when I started upstream, and I'd put it on when I was up on the knoll. It covered my .357 and most of the holster. At this point in the altercation I flipped my jacket back exposing the six-shooter; I hooked my thumb in my belt just ahead of the Magnum. I could see real trouble brewing fast and knew that I'd need a little help with these two.

When the Big Guy saw the yet holstered six-shooter he stopped and asked, "Can you use that, Buster?" I told him in a cold voice that I certainly could - and would - if the need arose. "A person would be a complete idiot to carry one and not be able to use it proficiently."

At this, the man in the boat, who hadn't said a word yet, cut in with, "HOLD it - EVERYBODY!" Then, "Someone is going to get hurt here in a minute and I DON'T think it's gonna' be the game warden. Warden, YOU tell me what you want us to do and I'll help you see that it's done. We're wrong, and we know it."

This sudden respect for the law, along with the sidearm I was packing, took the wind out of the two who had been confronting me.

I checked their licenses, issued the three men summonses and seized the sack of fish. Most of the trout were around sixteen inches long, and all were heavy with spawn.

That evening in Meeker I took the men before the Justice of the Peace. After hearing my testimony and giving each fisherman a chance to tell his side the Judge fined the one man willing to help me $50.00 and costs. The other two were fined $150.00 each and costs.

Chapter Nineteen

As I pulled the contents out of the envelope from the Wyoming Game Department I had my fingers crossed mentally. Sure enough! I had drawn an antelope permit for one of the areas in the southwestern part of the state. The season would open on the morning of September 12, and I planned on being in the field about daylight on that day.

After supper I called Jack Calver, a friend who lived in Meeker and intended to hunt with me if we both drew out on the permits. Jack informed me that he also had received a permit that same day.

The following weeks were used as time permitted in fine tuning my 7mm Mag. and getting my camper trailer outfitted and ready. Jack also burned up a lot of ammo and was preparing for the hunt.

For this hunt I planned to use a load I had worked up especially for antelope. The load is 150 grain Nosler partition bullet backed by 68 grains of 4831 and #200 C.C.I. primers. In my pre-64 Model 70 Winchester which I rebarreled years ago for the 7mm Remington Magnum bullet this load is deadly on pronghorns up to 400 yards. I like it extremely well because it doesn't explode when it connects like some of the softer bullets do from these fast, powerful calibers. It's also a top loading for any game from grizzly on down in my rifle. It's a hot load and I'm definitely not suggesting it as the load for anyone else; but I have had excellent results with it.

I sighted my rifle in to hit one inch high at 200 yards. Sighted in as such I can make a 350-yard shot on antelope rather easily. I prefer a standing broadside shot from the sitting position, if possible.

On the morning of September 11th, Jack met me at my home. We took two vehicles so if something happened to one we still would have an ace in the hole. We arrived at our destination late that afternoon and "set up camp" - a self-contained 21 foot camp trailer. (In the "olden" days I used an 8 x 10 foot wall tent on my antelope hunts!)

We saw a lot of antelope along the way that day with a high number of bucks. Some of them would run close to the 15-inch class. Ever since Jack and I had sent in our applications early that spring Jack had repeatedly said that he wanted to get a buck with 16-inch horns. It's not often that you run out and knock over a 16-inch buck. Far more often it will be in the 13-14 inch class at around 150-175 yards standing broadside, looking at the hunter.

Right after daylight the next morning I glanced

out the window of the camper and saw some antelope traveling along the top of the ridge about 200 yards from the trailer - the first game of opening day!

As soon as it was light enough to see well Jack and I "mounted up" in his Ford Bronco and headed out into the breaks. By noon we had seen a lot of game and passed up a total of 53 buck antelope! Some of them were quite respectable, but nothing I thought would make sixteen inches, nor the Boone and Crockett record book.

Jack was after a sixteen-incher and I was again out to try and get a buck that would go in the record book. I've tried this for many years. Although some of the bucks I've taken were darned good trophies, only one to date had made the records and that for less than the sixty-day shrinking period. By the time it qualified for measuring it had shrunk to just under the minimum score.

We found an elevated spot with a hill behind us so we wouldn't be skylined and ate our lunch. While eating lunch we counted around seventy antelope scattered around out in front of us. Following lunch I told Jack that I was going to take a mountain a-foot and see what I could scare up. As Jack wanted to work in closer to the "prairie goats" out in front of us I asked him to pick me up at a large spring area about three miles back at 5:00 p.m. I planned to spend the afternoon roaming over the side of the mountain. I've found that often the big bucks will head for the rough country after a few shots have been fired out in the flats.

By 4:00 p.m. I had looked over quite a few bucks, some that were tempting; but after really sizing them up I turned them down and eased on to the next ridge. About 4:30 I headed for the spring.

Not over a quarter mile from the spring area I saw two bucks and a doe walk up out of a large wash about 600 yards from me. At this same time I saw Jack pull up to the spring in his Bronco.

After taking a quick look at the bucks with my 10 x 40 binoculars I knew these were both darned good bucks. I grabbed my spotting scope out of my back pack, screwed it up to 35-power and looked the bucks over. Immediately I saw that the second one was one hell of a good buck. Not exceptionally long horns, but very heavy horns with large bases and heavy, long prongs. I didn't need a second look to make up my mind that I was going to try for a shot at this old fella'.

I slipped into the wash and made my way down as fast as possible. I knew the bucks had also seen Jack pull up to the spring and would soon head for the rough ground. I eased up behind a small sage bush on the bank of the wash to see what the antelope were doing. They had worked away from the wash and I realized that I wasn't going to get any closer.

As I slipped up out of the wash I was in - the antelope saw me. After three or four seconds they decided that they didn't want any part of me and started to trot off. Immediately I dropped to a sitting position - my favorite - took a quick estimate of the distance which I figured was just short of 300 yards. As I swung the cross-hairs with the base of the buck's neck I squeezed the trigger. The unmistakable "whump" of the Nosler hitting home!

I saw the buck lurch as I slammed another round up the tube of the Mag. Then, the buck folded up. The other buck and the doe headed for parts unknown.

I stepped off the distance to where the bullet had hit the target and came up with three hundred and one long steps. As soon as I was near the downed buck I knew that I had one hell of a trophy.

When I looked towards the spring I saw the Bronco headed my way. We took some pictures and rough-scored the head. It scored close to 85 Boone and Crockett points. Surely this head would easily make the book-even after the 60-day shrinking period.

(Here, though, a "P.S." is necessary. Unfortunately, for whatever unexplained reason, the taxidermist BOILED the head, shrinking it below the minimum for the records!)

The next morning Jack connected. His buck measured 15 5/8 inches on one side and an even 16 inches on the other! It is an excellent trophy, too.

Beginning with 1973, this antelope made the 23rd one-shot kill I've made with my old 7mm Mag. on big game animals.

Chapter Twenty

One time I asked a doctor friend who was my hunting partner if he believed that at times certain people went temporarily insane when hunting. Doc said that he had thought about this very subject, and had come up with about the same conclusion I had.

This is a terrible thing to say or think, but some of the actions I've seen and experienced leave me with this impression. The following episode will explain why.

As quite often happened, one fall there was a full moon the first part of hunting season which made the average hunting tough. Game animals like deer and elk do more feeding at night during moonlight and "hole up" tighter during regular daylight hours.

Also, at this time of year the White River deer migration was on. Of course, the moonlight nights increase the night-time migration of the deer.

Lots of hunters who can't get their deer during daylight hours turn to spotlight hunting along the roads. This type is not a true sportsman or hunter. He is one of the human slobs that gives the sport a black eye. But, this type of person is apt to be encountered everywhere we go.

I soon discovered after three or four days of patrolling during that hunting season that the spotlighters were at it again. I found numerous empty rifle cartridges along the roads and several places where deer had been killed. Immediately I began to do a lot of night patrolling.

Quite often in those days some of us wardens would take our wives along for company and to help keep us awake. After several days of patrolling all day and most of the night is was very hard to stay awake until midnight or 2:00 a.m., or whenever.

Right after dark one night I asked my wife if she wanted to accompany me on patrol and see how the deer were migrating. Of course, she said "yes", and we were on our way. We headed east out of Meeker to the Little Beaver Creek area, then swung north to the Coal Creek area, up this to Nine Mile Gulch, which brought us out to Nine Mile Pass north of Meeker. We had seen some deer heading west, but surprisingly, however, we hadn't met a single auto.

I told my wife that it didn't look like much was going to happen that night, so we might as well go home. I'd get a good early start in the morning.

When we got down to within six miles of Meeker a small three-point buck ran up on the highway in front of us, across the road, and lay down on the right-hand shoulder of the road. At first I thought the little buck was hurt; but apparently he was just tired. I snapped my spotlight on him so we could get a good look at him. Although I could see no blood he had his mouth open. Evidently he had been running for some reason and needed a "breather".

I said to my wife that I had better run the deer off the road before some nut came by and shot him right in front of us. I asked her to get out and come around the pickup to work the spotlight from the outside of the truck as it would be easier to keep the light on the buck and I'd try to work him down the fence to a low place where he could jump and be off the highway.

I no more than got these words out of my mouth when a set of headlights appeared around a curve down towards Meeker. I said, "Hold it a minute and let this car get by." As I said this I turned on my red light to alert the driver to be cautious. Just before the car was even with the deer the little buck jumped up and just stood there. I still had the spotlight on it as I hoped that this would hold the deer where he was and keep him from running out in front of the car to get hit broadside.

The car pulled a few feet past us and stopped. I assumed that they just wanted to look at the buck since my lights lit it up.

I was watching the deer; my wife was watching the car. Their dome light was on and she could see someone reaching in the back seat. "They're getting a gun out of the back!" she exclaimed.

"Oh, I doubt if they're diggin' out a rifle; probably after a camera to get a picture," I replied. "No one would be damned fool enough to shoot a deer on the highway at 10:00 o'clock at night - in the game warden's light!"

"O.K., gal; jump out and work the light for me while I get this little buck off the road." As I started to open my door Shirley started to open hers and step out, at the same time looking back toward the car.

Suddenly it sounded like the whole world blew up in our ears! The cab of the pickup lit up from the muzzle flash - the buck hit the ground and my wife screamed, "My God! They're shooting at you!"

Instantly I knew what had happened. Sure enough - one of the two people in the car had gotten a rifle out - and shot the deer - barely missing Shirley.

In just a few long strides I was back to the shooter who was working the bolt to run another round into the chamber. I grabbed the rifle barrel, giving it a twist, jerking the gun away from him. "What the hell do you think you're doing?" I demanded.

"Oh, I won't argue with you, Mister; you go ahead and take the deer. I just wanted the fun of shootin' it," he answered quickly. I told the guy who I was and, "Get up there in the lights of the pickup where I can watch you!"

I asked, "What does a blinking red light mean to you?" He replied, "Well...I dunno'...some kind of danger, I guess."

"Exactly!" I agreed.

The man said that he didn't think about the flashing red light; just thought I didn't have guts enough to shoot the buck! We walked back to where he was standing when he shot. It was about twelve feet back of my pickup and about two and a half feet from the right-hand door. If Shirley had stepped out a couple of seconds sooner very possibly she would have been hit in the back with a 30-06 bullet.

When I told the man that I was taking him back to Meeker and throwing him in jail overnight he said, "You aren't giving me much of a chance!" I countered, "You sure as hell didn't give that little buck any chance, and you almost shot my wife at the same time!"

Then he asked me if I ever took a drink. "Yes, at times I do; but I'm particular who I drink with - and I never drink while on duty," I said.

"Well, Warden, I have a fifth of Scotch in the car. I'll give you fifty dollars and the bottle of Scotch. You take them and the deer and go to Meeker - and, I'll head for the eastern slope." I reminded him that, on top of everything else, this was bribery and that he, the buck and all were going to Meeker - one way or another.

While following him into town my opinion of him fell a few points lower, if possible, when he ran over a cottontail rabbit.

He was thrown in jail, with his auto parked at the courthouse where the sheriff took custody of the car keys. The man's friend stayed at a motel.

The next day the shooter went to court and paid a $300.00 fine plus costs. In those days there was no point system; so nothing could be done about his future hunting rights. However, he wasn't eligible to shoot another deer that season.

This was just one example I've seen where a person lost all good judgment while hunting. So, I ask: IS it temporary insanity?

Chapter Twenty-One

One fall, during big game hunting season, Joe Papez was assigned to work with me for a while. He was Superintendent of the Bel-Aire Rearing Ponds, but he always enjoyed helping the game wardens. He and I got along well and I liked him. He had good common sense and would hold up his end of any job he undertook.

We put in three or four days on general patrol and made a few cases, but none of them were out of the ordinary. All the time Joe kept wishing that he could get in on one of the big cases. I'd tell him to just hang in there and have patience; no doubt we would run into something that would fulfill his wishes.

After working these few days I told him that the next morning we would head down into the Piceance

Creek area west of Meeker and see how things were going. The next morning we hit Piceance Creek and worked along to the Yellow Creek road. We ate lunch on top of the divide between Piceance and Yellow Creeks.

We checked out several camps and a good number of hunters. The hunting was good and there were deer hanging in all of the camps. We hadn't found anything wrong up to that time, however.

About 2:00 p.m. Joe said that he sure wished that we could get some excitement going. "I'll tell you what we might do," I said. "I know a big gulch up ahead where there are usually two or three big camps of non-residents; so let's drive up there and see how things are."

After turning up the big gulch we didn't go far until we came to a larger than usual camp with six or eight tents, a generator, a couple of large refrigerators and all the trimmings to make a very comfortable camp. As I recall there were eleven men in the "settlement" - nine hunters and two help.

When we pulled up and stopped we received some cool glances. I told Joe to keep his eyes peeled and his ears open as I expected to find some violations here.

We introduced ourselves and were invited into the big tent that served as a cook shack, dining and "living" rooms. I told them that we wanted to check all licenses and the game they had taken.

That fall there was a two-deer area which season was in effect at the same time as the one-deer season. The dividing line between the two areas was the divide between Piceance Creek and Roan Creek. This boundary was a good ten miles south of that particular camp. It was lawful for a hunter to take his first deer anywhere he wished; but the second one had to be taken in the two-deer area. It was completely legal to take both deer in the two-deer area; but, not two deer north of the aforementioned boundary.

The nine hunters claimed that they had taken their first deer in the Piceance Creek area, and the second ones in the two deer area. I told them that we wanted to check the carcasses; from their actions I knew that something was wrong.

As we walked down to a big wash below their camp a couple hundred yards I eased over to Joe and, in a low voice, I told him to stay up on top and watch things; I would go down in the wash and look the deer carcasses over. They had done a beautiful job of caring for the meat, and all the animals were tagged properly.

After I climbed out of the wash Joe winked at me and nodded his head towards the divide. When everyone gathered at the big tent again I asked them who was in charge of the camp. At first no one wanted to be the "Head Honcho" of the outfit, but finally a rather big man said, "I guess I am." I then told them that I thought they had killed most, if not all, of the second deer in the Piceance Creek area. (I know this area as well as any man and to get to the two-deer area some ten miles away - as the crow flies - you would have to drive halfway again over a poor, very poor, jeep road. Then, more than likely you would have to drop down onto the south side of the divide and that could be several miles farther.)

I told the "CEO" to pick some of the group to go with him. We were going to take a trip. I said that I wanted to see for myself just where the second deer were killed. In reply he said that he couldn't show me all the places, but he could show me where he killed his. He said that it was too late to make the trip up there this evening, that he would take us up there "tomorrow". No, I told him; we are going right now, and if he pulled any funny stuff I'd call extra help to come in on the deal at which time he could expect the worst. Or - he could cooperate and we'd give them all the consideration possible.

We all took off - they in a jeep and Joe and I following in my unit. For about twenty minutes they kept ahead as if they knew where they were going. Joe asked, "Do you suppose we're wrong about them?" I didn't think so and soon we'd know because the jeep road we were following forked up ahead. One branch would lead to the east, then back south and to the divide. The other turned to the right and to a dead end on an old oil well site some four miles ahead.

When we reached the forks the jeep came to a stop. We pulled up behind them and everyone got out. The hunters walked back to meet us. I said, "Well, what's the trouble?" The leader made one more attempt to sway us to his side. He pointed up the jeep tracks leading through the cedars to the right and said that they had killed the deer up there a mile or two. I told him that he would have to show us an actual kill site and the leavings from dressing out the deer. At this time the other hunter said, "Oh, hell; we can't fool these guys. Let's tell 'em the truth and quit playin' games."

I assured them that we would recommend to the Judge that he assess the minimum fine due to their cooperation.

We returned to the camp, gave nine hunters summonses and loaded up eighteen deer carcasses. Actually, since one deer was obviously illegal, it made both deer illegal.

These hunters appeared in court the next day and were fined $200.00 and costs each. I requested that the Judge permit each of them to have one of their deer released back to them due to their cooperation - after they found that the "jig" was up.

As we walked out of the courthouse after the trial I asked Joe, "Well, has that granted your wish to get in on a big one?" "That'll do 'til we find a bigger one," he replied.

For the next three or four years this group of hunters would never fail to look me up and ask about hunting. I was glad to see them and especially appreciated their attitude. I always tried my best to help them in any way I could.

Chapter Twenty-Two

One summer, along in early July, Bill Roland, the game warden who had the Craig district called from his headquarters and related some poaching going on in the high country. It involved people at a small sawmill. He wanted to "shake" the mill down and said that he'd like to have me help him if he could get an O.K. from our mutual supervisor. I told Bill that I would be glad to assist. He and I got along very well and worked together every chance we could. Our supervisor gave us the go-ahead on the shake-down.

We laid our plans and the next day I met Bill; then we drove up to the sawmill site. When we arrived there we learned that all but one man and his wife had gone to Craig for one reason or another. The one lone couple there lived on above the mill in a little two-room slab shack.

By the time we had looked the mill itself over, and found nothing out of line we decided to question this one employee as much as possible to see what we could learn from him. After about twenty minutes of talking to the guy we were quite sure that he had some illegal elk meat stashed some place.

Finally after making a thorough search of the area around his cabin we decided that it had to be in the cabin. The man's wife was in the cabin, and he claimed that she was sick in bed. We didn't believe this and told him so. I'm sure that the lady could hear us through the thin walls of the cabin.

The man kept telling us that our warrant wasn't any good after sundown and since his wife was sick in bed there was no way we could search the cabin. There was NO question in my mind about entering that cabin under the circumstances! Just the same, we were sure that the guy had illegal meat and we were going to try to find it.

Bill and I got off to the side a little ways and decided on a plan to "smoke" this old boy out. We told him - in loud voices that we were sure the lady could hear - that Bill was going to stay there and I'd drive down to the nearest ranch and get the lady at the ranch to return with me as a "matron" and that she would be deputized so she could enter and look for the meat. (I assumed that the woman in the cabin would hop in bed with the meat, thereby making it absolutely "Off Limits" to get the elk meat. And, frankly, I didn't know if I could find some woman to act in our behalf; but it was worth a try.)

As I turned and started walking toward Bill's

pickup I heard a door open. I looked around to see the woman just stepping out of the cabin door with a package in her hands... As she tossed the bundle down next to her husband she said, "Give 'em the damned meat! Maybe, then, they'll leave us alone!"

We summoned the man into court at Craig. From then on we didn't hear any more about illegal hunting in that area for the rest of the summer.

This is the same summer that I became acquainted with George (Mike) Michaely, an energetic, likeable sort of guy who'd moved here from out of state and had bought a riverfront resort east of Meeker. He called his place Tru-Sport Lodge, and became active right away in his hunting and fishing operations.

I'd met Mike one day while checking fishermen and we became quite good friends. I would stop by his outfit often on the way up the river, or, if I wasn't in too much of a hurry going down stream I'd stop and shoot the bull with him. We got to the point where we did quite a lot of bird hunting together; we just plain hit it off.

One day while talking to Mike he asked me if I would drop in the next day some time and check every fisherman of his that I could find. He had been told that some of them were catching as many as they could - in some instances exceeding the legal bag limit considerably: like two or three times the legal number!

About the middle of the afternoon the following day I stopped at Mike's. He was down by the river where several of his guests were fishing. I followed the trail down to the river where Mike motioned toward a lawn chair and said, "Have a seat; I'll point out one person that needs a good scare." He nodded towards a lady fishing perhaps a hundred yards from us. He said that he knew she had caught a limit of fish before noon and now she was catching more.

I told Mike I'd go check the lady and see if I could "smoke her out" since Mike had told me that this gal and her husband were going to leave that evening and return to their home.

I hoped to spook her enough that she and her husband would pull out earlier than expected; I'd intercept their auto and make a shake-down, hoping to find the surplus fish, if any. If I'd had a search warrant for them I could have just searched their cabin; that would have made it simple. But, to obtain one now I'd have to drive to Meeker, round up the Justice of the Peace, have him issue the warrant, drive back to Mike's and by this time she and her husband might be gone.

I got up and walked down to where she was dippin' a worm in the water. She was doing fine, too. I told her who I was and asked her for her license. She produced the license; I took the information I needed, then asked her how many fish she had. She said that she needed two more to fill her limit.

"Did you fish this morning, and - if so - how many did you catch then?" I asked. "Oh, yes; I fished this morning, but I only caught one little fish," she replied.

"Do you have any fish at the cabin?" "No, we've eaten all the fish we've caught - until right now," was her answer. "Thank you, Mam; I suppose you know that one day's limit is all you are allowed in one day." I saw her expression change, and knew something wasn't quite right. I checked the rest of the fishermen that I could see, then walked back over to where Mike was.

The lady had quit fishing while I was checking the other fishermen, and had gone back in her cabin. Mike asked me what I thought and I told him I'd bet and give odds that the woman had too many fish.

None of Mike's cabins were modern so everyone had to use a central bath house-wash room. We were sitting there discussing the matter when all of a sudden Mike - who was facing this couple's cabin - interrupted his other remarks and said, "Hey, something is going on!"

I turned around to look in the direction of their cabin. There was the fisherwoman - almost to the ladies' bathroom - carrying a pan probably 9 x 16 x 2 in size, with a dish towel covering it. My thoughts were, "OH, HELL! She's gonna' flush the extra fish down the 'John' - and there's nothing I can do about it! I sure can't go in THERE and grab the fish!"

Boy, did Mike ever get a bang out of that! Personally, I couldn't see anything funny about it; however, since then I look back and see how the gal used her head.

Anyway, we watched to see what would happen next. In a couple of minutes she came out - without the pan - and went back into her cabin. Mike and I both figured that since she didn't have the pan she had just left it in there until the coast was clear, then she'd retrieve her fish.

"Mike, we've got to find some woman who will go in there and see what she did with the pan and the fish." He jumped up and said, "Wait here; I've got an idea. There's a gal up at the house who'll go down and check things out for us."

I waited where I was. No time was wasted; he disappeared into the house and in a few minutes he came out and joined me again down by the river. Soon after that a lady walked out of the house and down into a cabin. "That's the gal," Mike said. The woman came back out of the cabin and walked to the bathroom. In a little while she came back out and then over to us. Mike introduced her to me, and asked her if she had found the fish. She said that the pan and tea towel were there; but, no fish. She had checked the reservoir on the toilet, behind the hot water heater, and any place where they might have been hidden, but no dice. Apparently, as I suspected might happen, the fish had been flushed down the "John", leaving no "corpus delicti" for me.

This was one of the few times when I had to admit defeat; however, I couldn't help but admire her technique to beat the law.

Of course, Mike didn't forget this episode either for quite a while.

Chapter Twenty-Three

On the evening of August 31, 1972, two other hunters and I loaded our gear on the plane which would fly us to Stevens Lake on the headwaters of the Nisling River in the Yukon Territory. At this point we met our guides, cook and horse jingler for the up-coming mixed bag hunt. We camped there that night with plans to get an early start the next day.

Morning found a long procession of us - riders and pack horses - winding our way downstream to our base camp some twelve to fifteen miles away. This was the fourth day after a week of almost steady rain which had swollen the river and the side streams to flood stage. Naturally, this made the bogs in the river valley much deeper than usual, causing a considerable number of detours to reach the higher and more solid ground.

To the newcomer - or "cheechako" - riding into one of these bogs is to experience a feeling of impending disaster as the saddle horse sinks deeper - and deeper - into the mire. Rarely, however, does a horse get completely down in one. To me it is very interesting to watch a horse that is an "Old Hand" at bogs in the North country negotiate the crossing of one when given his head. He uses small clumps of grass, willows, or anything to step on that might help buoy him up a little. Horses that aren't accustomed to bogs will have a tendency to flounder and splash on through.

On the way into camp we crossed the route taken by an early day cattle drive into the gold camps in the Prospector Mountain area. Originally the steers were shipped by boat to Burwash Landing. They were unloaded at this point and trailed overland to the gold camps. This was quite a feat to accomplish, then or now. I was told that only one steer was lost, and that was due to the bogs. In those days the Yukon was crammed full of the big northern wolf; but no steers were lost to their predation. Perhaps the wolves preferred moose meat.

On the way in we saw one wolf and many moose and caribou tracks along the trail. The next morning the other two hunters and their guides headed back upstream while my guide, Fred, and I headed downstream to scout for Dall rams. Along the trail we saw fresh wolf sign and several more moose tracks as well as a fresh grizzly track. According to the grizzly's track he was a big bear that had done considerable feeding on tender roots of the young willows and blueberry bushes it had "plowed" up with its long-clawed forefeet. At times there would be patches of ground the size of a large room dug up by the bear to get at these roots. It reminded me of a garden space that had been spaded for planting.

After three hours of riding Fred spotted a Dall ram lying up in some scrub evergreens and rocks across the river. Fred is an easy-going, keen-eyed, very interesting person. He has guided and packed across most of British Columbia and the Yukon; he doesn't seem to hurry, but he makes every move count. We set up the spotting scope and looked the ram over. He turned out to be about a 34-incher. A beautiful animal, but nothing to spend more time on. Let him complete his growth.

After another couple of miles we spotted twelve more sheep, low on a hillside across the river. These sheep were a considerable distance below the shale slides and the rocky ledges higher up on the mountain. We immediately checked them out and found that they were all rams. They ranged from three-quarter curls to old adult rams. Two of the larger rams looked like they would exceed the magical forty-inch mark.

These sheep had collected around a mineral lick which apparently was used by a lot of animals in this area as there were eight trails leading into the lick. The lick had undoubtedly been used for countless years because a huge area had been eaten away by the area wildlife. I've seen and examined numerous licks in the States and in British Columbia; but never have I seen one larger than this one in the Yukon Territory.

The rams were well over a mile from us, out in a

clearing on the hillside, enabling them to see us - unless we used care in our movements. So, we made a big detour to get closer for a better look. We tied our horses in a heavy stand of spruce, then set up the spotting scope to really check them out. Three of the rams were fine trophies in anyone's book. The two largest heads no doubt exceeded forty inches around the curl, with heavy bases.

We ate our lunch and watched these sheep until they fed and worked their way back up over the ridge. We didn't try to get a shot at any one of them, although we could have stalked to the edge of the river and made a roughly 300-yard shot. We would still be on the wrong side of the river which was really high!

After the sheep disappeared Fred said, "Well, we have to find a way to cross this 'damned crick' - and from the looks of the high water we're going to have to swim the horses across." He asked me if I was game to do so, and if I had ever ridden a swimming horse. I said, "Hell, yes; as a kid we used to swim horses across the Yampa River that flowed through our ranch in Colorado just for fun. Besides, if it means getting a "poke" at one of those big rams I'd swim the river WITHOUT a horse - or, even try floating across!"

Since we figured the sheep would stay close to where we last saw them we started working downstream looking for a spot to cross. Most of the river bank was set up so that either you could get in the water okay - but it was too high to get out on the other side; or, just the reverse. Finally, we found a place where we could enter the water and the horses could get out on the other side.

We loosened the cinches, shucked our chaps and saddlebags and pulled a plastic sack up over the bottom part of my rifle scabbard to keep the water out. Then we swam the horses across and after a couple of lunges up the bank we were out of the river and onto dry ground. Returning to the other side of the river we practiced one more crossing, just to make sure we would be able to get in and out okay the next day. We cinched up, grabbed our chaps and saddlebags and headed for camp, soaked to the belt by water that had slopped up into our saddles.

(Anyone swimming a saddle horse should remember - for their own safety - if they get into trouble during the swim they ought to grab the horse's tail. If possible, never roll or fall into the water on the downstream side of the horse because you could be dragged under the horse in its swimming efforts.)

After supper, when comparing notes of the day's hunt, we learned that both Dick and Flay had been on good rams, but the stalks turned out badly for both of them. Neither one had connected; however, spirits were running high as a lot of sheep had been seen by the three pairs of hunters and their guides. There was no doubt in any of our minds that we would get a chance at a very good ram sooner or later.

The next morning an early start from camp put us at the crossing around 10:00 a.m. We had checked for the rams a good mile away, and found that nine head, including the big ones, were back near the lick. We swam the horses across, again leaving chaps and saddlebags on the bank to be picked up on our return. After across the river we headed for high ground.

About four hundred yards from the lick was a rocky point that jutted out above the surrounding poplars and brush. It gave us a good view of the lick and most of the trails converging on it. We eased out on this point and set up the spotting scope to check the heads. The six three-quarter curl rams were getting ready to pull out, working in our direction. The three big ones were bedded down near the lick, but, no doubt, would follow the other six soon. Fred and I both figured we could reach a brushy knoll some two hundred yards from them. The shot would have to be made from that point, if we could reach it before the rams moved out.

I suggested slipping a round in the chamber of my 7mm Mag. Since the cover we would have to stalk through was fairly thick and the sheep were apparently headed in our direction this seemed like a good idea. Fred hadn't been with me long enough to know how I'd react to the situation and the stalk, so he vetoed the idea of putting a round in the chamber. Right then he didn't know that I had outfitted and guided deer and elk hunters for several years myself.

About half-way to the knoll we suddenly saw the six smaller rams lying about sixty yards to our right. Fortunately they were looking the other way and possibly dreaming of the time when they would rate at the top of the "pecking order" of wild rams. The wind was in our favor and we were slipping along almost as quiet as shadows, so the rams didn't even look our way. A quick nod between us and we moved to our left, out of sight of the rams. After this we were really on our toes, and - as if by magic - the three big rams appeared in front of us at about seventy five yards; they were heading almost straight at us!

Probably the reason we weren't immediately discovered by the sheep was due to the second ram in line; he was butting the leader in the fanny every two or three steps and the third one was occupied watching this action. Every time the leader received a butt from the second ram he would half turn to face the trouble coming from behind him.

Although it seemed like it took ages to chamber a round in my rifle, and size up the three rams, it took only seconds to decide that the leader was the best. Fred eased out of the line of fire while I sighted in on the leader's shoulder as he turned to face his antagonist after another rear-end wallop. Then I squeezed 'er off. The blast sent the big ram reeling backwards and his two partners scattering like scalded cats. About four jumps and the old boy piled up for good.

The ram that had been doing the butting ran off about a hundred yards and stopped. As he looked back at the downed leader we could see that he, too, had over a full curl. However, the left horn had a big chunk missing from the top of the curl. This was probably due to fighting as the horns absorb a tremendous amount of shock when the rams crash together during their fighting.

After looking the twelve-year-old ram over and putting a tape to the horns I was sure that this old monarch of the peaks and shale slides would place in the record book after the sixty day shrinkage period. The head was very impressive with the longest horn going over forty-one inches. Several months later it was measured for a score of 173 1/8 points and ranks 137th in the Tenth Edition of the Boone and Crockett record book listing 264 Dall sheep.

We took pictures and caped out the head. Then we hung what meat we couldn't take with us; it would be picked up the next day. Now it was time to head back to camp via the swim across the river.

When taking a ram like this one the wet saddle and the black flies didn't dispel any of the wonders of this vast country with its unpolluted air and water, and chain after chain of beautiful mountains.

As we rode along I couldn't help but wonder how the rest of the hunt would go. Next we would start hunting for grizzly and moose.

Chapter Twenty-Four

Wall Lake is one of the many lakes situated on the Flat Tops and is an excellent native trout producer. In fact, the outlet water from it spills over the rim of the Flat Tops above Trappers Lake and forms one of the main inlets to Trappers. For years Wall Lake was in my district, so I patrolled it as well as Trappers Lake.

One day I hiked up to the lake to check fishermen and while talking to a man after checking his license, and some very nice native trout, I noticed a flash across the lake - like the flash from a mirror. I asked the fisherman if he had seen that, too. He said that he hadn't. About that same time, though, we both saw another bright flash. I said, more to myself than to anyone, "If I didn't know better I'd say that was the flash from an auto windshield." The man I was talking to replied, "I would, too; but no one has ever been up here with any kind of an automobile 'cause there ain't no roads up here."

I thanked the guy for showing his license and the fish, then walked around to the other side of the lake where the flash came from. To my utter amazement I found a young guy unloading some camping gear from a jeep! He was backed into some timber near the water's edge.

I introduced myself, then asked him how he had managed to drive over the Flat Tops to this point. He said that he had driven up to Deep Lake, then followed the Government horse trail from "Indian Camp" to the Shingle Peak area, then west across the top to Wall Lake!

Prior to this incident I know of two jeeps that had been rolled trying to follow the horse trail from Indian Camp to the rim of the Flat Tops. One man was killed and the other had his back broken as the result of that endeavor. Due partly to these two accidents the Forest Service passed a regulation that outlawed any motorized mechanism within the Wilderness Area boundaries. The Flat Tops as well as Wall Lake are part of this Wilderness area.

I advised the fellow of this law and "jumped down his throat" about cutting the country up with jeep tracks which would, without a doubt, cause a lot of erosion in places. This possibility was almost certain to happen as the top soil on the Flat Tops is very thin, or shallow, and usually not over four inches deep. Then, in the wet areas or on the inclines the jeep tires would cut through this thin layer causing erosion to start soon due to the run-off of rain and melting snow.

After informing him of what he was up against he loaded his camping gear and left.

A few days later I hauled my saddle and pack horses up to Trappers Lake. The following day I got an early start and tracked the jeep all the way to Indian Camp. I made a two day trip out of this and took quite a few slide pictures of places where the jeep had made deep ruts. In some places it had cut as deep as six to seven inches. I made a "log" of this so I could refer to it later.

The next summer at about the same time I had encountered the jeep driver at Wall Lake I took a group made up of Forest Service personnel and Game Department men over this same route, from Wall Lake to Indian Camp. We inspected the places where the worst ruts had been made the summer before and found that some of them were now fourteen to sixteen inches deep - and ten to twelve inches wide! This was the erosion in just one year!

Later that summer the Forest Service erected a large sign at Indian Camp warning the public of closed access to the Wilderness Area by motorized vehicles. To my knowledge no other jeeps ever made this trip.

While on the subject of Wall Lake, here is another experience:

One summer some of the biologists in both the Game Department and the Forest Service wanted to make a study of range conditions on the Flat Tops around the Wall Lake - Shingle Peak areas. Since this was all in my district I wanted to see what was going on, too.

The group was made up consisting of seventeen Game and Fish and Forest Service personnel, two men from Meeker to do the packing and cooking, and I joined the group. Camp was set up near Wall Lake.

(Incidentally, the White River National Forest is the second oldest national forest in the United States, having been established October 16, 1891, by President Benjamin Harrison. The oldest is the Shoshone in Wyoming, on the eastern side of Yellowstone National Park.)

I noticed two other fishing camps set up within 200 yards of us, but didn't talk with any of the "residents" that day. Since it was evening by the time our camp was pitched and the horses cared for it was too late to make any kind of a ride to check on range conditions. So, we elected to try our luck fishing. We would have an hour and a half before supper, so everyone except the two men who were doing the cooking headed for the lake.

By the time supper was ready I had caught my limit of fish - six natives that weighed an average of two pounds each. In those days the limit was ten fish or ten pounds and one fish, whichever you acquired first.

In addition to us there was one other fisherman who was fishing from a rubber boat. I saw him catch four nice big natives and when I poled my rickety log raft to shore and headed for camp he was still at it.

For the next three days we left camp right after breakfast and rode all day, checking range conditions, getting back to our camp late in the evenings. We didn't get in any more fishing during those three days. On the evening of the third day of riding the boss from Denver made the statement that the following day would be a day of rest and fishing. Each evening when we returned to camp the man with the rubber raft would be out fishing.

Since I was the game warden over this area and was expected to check so many licenses each month I advised the men that I wanted to check their fishing licenses after supper - including the Director of the Department. All of these men had fished the first evening. Also, I wanted to check that fisherman with the rubber raft.

After supper everyone produced a valid fishing license except Larry, one of the "Big Guns" from Denver. The rest of the men really poured it on him, and kiddingly kept telling me to give him a ticket - that he hadn't bought a license yet. He claimed he had one all right, but just couldn't find it. Of course, I had to produce my license along with the rest of them. I told Larry I'd give him until 6:00 p.m. the following day to find his license; if he couldn't I was going to give him a summons. With the Director there I knew he would have to back me up and Larry also knew this.

The next day did not turn out to be our "day of rest" - and "fishing" as earlier planned. Instead, the day was spent riding and looking at the range. We did manage to get back to camp about 5:00 p.m. though, and poor old Larry had really taken a ribbing from the gang. He even asked me off to the side if I'd really give him a ticket if he couldn't find his license. My only choice would be to issue him a citation for fishing without a license! And he knew that I would, too.

When we rode back into camp that evening Larry tied his horse to a tree and went to his tent, starting to dig through his belongings - looking for the license he claimed that he had. In about ten minutes he let out a whoop and came out of his tent waving his fishing license! I checked it for him right then and there.

After taking care of my saddle horse I headed around the lake to check the lad in the rubber boat. As I walked around to a point where I could talk to the man I asked him to paddle over to me, which he did.

When he reached the shore I told him who I was and asked him for his license. He looked at me, then out across the lake, and said, "Mister, I don't have a license."

I could hardly believe my ears! This man had been fishing EVERY day of the four days we'd been camped there. He said that he knew who we were, but after the first evening when no one asked him for a license he figured that we weren't interested in him. On top of having no license I discovered at his camp almost twice the number of trout which were legal. The fellow was summoned into court in Meeker.

I suggested to Larry that he trade places with the fisherman so he would know what he missed by finding his license. To this proposal he told me to go "someplace where it is nice and warm".

Chapter Twenty-Five

"Hi, William; this is Cleve." That was the response to my "hello" when I answered the telephone. "Can you drop out in a few minutes?" "Sure, Cleve; I'll be right out."

I was working on reports; the paper work had to be done as well as the patrolling. Usually it had to be "worked in", so to speak. I got rid of that disgusting activity real quick by walking out of my home office and closing the door behind me.

There was a short pre-deer season opening in a couple of days down in the Browns Park - Cold Spring Mountain area. The warden from Craig whose district this area was in wanted to throw in a road block at the Sunbeam bridge. Sunbeam is a very small community located about seventy miles west of Craig. Practically all of the traffic coming out of the Browns Park area passes over this bridge and through Sunbeam, headed for Craig, usually.

The story I'm going to tell to the reader of this book has been picked up and told several times as if it happened in a different locality, with different people involved. I have also seen it in print - in a wildlife magazine - and even in a book in my personal library, where on page seven the event is described as occurring elsewhere, and attributed to a game warden whose name is absolutely foreign to me! This episode, however, is a matter of record, and can be verified by any of the remaining participants.

Bill Roland, the Craig warden, Kenny Fullenwider, the Rangely warden and I, together with our wives all met at a small log cabin which would serve as our "headquarters" while we were running the road block. We intended to run this "block" from 3:00 p.m. until midnight. Our wives would get supper for us and keep the coffee pot going for the next eight or nine hours.

Bill had gotten word that quite a bit of game law violation had taken place in this area the past year, and felt that it would happen again this year. In addition, he had picked up information concerning a group of hunters who intended to get in a little Canada goose hunting in addition to the legal deer hunting. The Browns Park area is quite a good goose sanctuary and two of the hunters in this party were real dyed-in-the-wool goose hunters.

We would wait in the cabin, which was only a few yards from the bridge. When we would see a car coming, which was possible for three-quarters of a mile, we would walk up to the end of the bridge and if they were hunters we'd check them out for game, licenses, etc.

By dark we had picked up three or four violations. One hunter had shot two sage chickens in addition to a deer. He was given a summons for the illegal possession of two sage grouse. The other two or three violations were failure to tag their deer.

About 9:00 p.m. we saw headlights appear at the far end of this three-quarter mile stretch of road. We grabbed our flashlights and walked up to the bridge. When the car was about 200 yards from the bridge we turned on the red lights on one of the pickups that we had positioned for this purpose after dark.

When the car stopped Bill, who knew the occupants, as did Ken and I, said, "Hi, Guys; we are checking all hunters out of this area - and their game." As he looked up at the head of a two-point which was exposed from under a tarp covering the rest of the deer and the entire luggage rack on top of the car, he nodded to Ken and me.

Right away we could see that all of the men were a little nervous; so we figured something was wrong. Ken asked who claimed the buck and when the owner spoke up, Ken asked him for his license, continuing, "We would like to check all of your licenses." While he and Bill were doing this I was looking around the car, especially the hub caps as this was a possible hideout for any kind of grouse. Over the years I had found grouse on three different occasions in hub caps.

When Bill and Kenny had checked the licenses Bill started checking inside the car and Ken had stepped up on the running board of this older model auto used mainly for hunting. He was going to check the little buck for tagging while I was talking to one of the hunters. I saw Bill straighten up beside the right hand side of the car and motion with his head for me to come and join him. I walked over and asked him what he had found.

"Turn your light on the shelf above the back seat; there's an open box of 12-gauge shells up there," was his reply. I did so and, sure enough, there were the shells!

In a low voice Bill said, "I'm sure they have been hunting geese; so let's really give this outfit a good looking over." With this Bill started pulling a couple of sleeping bags out of the car. Meanwhile, I walked around behind the auto and turned my flashlight up on the luggage rack, then went on around to where Ken was just finishing writing down the information he needed from the tag on the deer.

As I stepped up on the running board beside him I noticed one of the men had walked over so he could see what Ken and I were doing. I asked Ken if he had looked under the tarp. He said "no", but that he would. I jerked a knot loose on the rope holding the tarp fast to the rack and threw the tarp back, exposing most of the deer's body.

For some reason the set-up just looked too "pat" - handy for the deer's head to be checked and the tag positioned so it could be seen without undoing the tarp. This wasn't natural for most hunters.

As I started to shine my light under the tarp and over the buck I saw about an inch of a goose wing feather sticking out of where the brisket had been split on the buck when he was gutted. I jabbed Ken in the ribs and said, "Hey, look what I've found!"

I lifted the top side of the buck's ribs - exposing the goose inside the rib cavity. I took hold of the goose by one wing and pulled it out. Then I walked over and tossed it down in front of the car where the lights shone on it. All eyes were on the goose, of course, while I asked, "Which one of you did that?"

One of the men exclaimed, "Now WHERE did you find that GOOSE?" I answered, "Stuffed in that BUCK!"

The hunter's reply has become legendary as he snorted, "WELL! - that goose-eatin' son-of-a-bitch! He musta' swallered that goose while swimmin' the river!"

Naturally, none of them wanted to take the blame for the illegal goose. But, when they found out that we could charge all of them under a Federal warrant for illegal possession of a migratory waterfowl, the man who had speculated on the deer's appetite for goose admitted to the shooting. After this discovery we really shook the outfit down, but couldn't find anything else wrong.

The man who admitted shooting the goose was summoned into court in Craig where he was fined $100.00 plus costs for illegally shooting a goose. Federal charges were not filed on him.

Two or three years later I picked up one of these same men for illegally shooting a bull elk.

Another case where some people just don't give a tinker's damn about game laws.

Chapter Twenty-Six

Fall rolled around again and my local boss assigned another Department man to patrol the high country with me. In the past two or three years the men assigned had wanted to quit me after a day or two of patrolling on horseback. But, this fellow had his own saddle horse and pack horse. He promised that he would ride with me even if it was to be for all season.

Well, Joe Papez heard about the forthcoming event and asked me if he could go along, too. He said that he might not be the best cook, but he would keep the wood box full, pack all the water and wash the dishes. As for horses - he admitted that he had only a nodding acquaintance with them, but he would sure try to keep up. To cap off his resume, he said that he knew some good jokes that he thought we'd get a kick out of, and he'd try to think up some more. Now, with recommendations like those, how could I refuse? He was accepted to go along.

By this time I had several horses of my own; so I told Joe he could use one of them, a pinto that was as gentle as a dog.

We arrived at the cabin on the third evening before season, settled in and awaited morning for our first full day of patrolling.

The following day found us leaving the cabin at 6:00 a.m. We made a full day of it, arriving back at the cabin when it was almost dark. Poor Joe was so sore he could hardly stand after he slid from the saddle, but he never once uttered a complaint. Most of the hunters we encountered were just packing in; and we didn't run into any violations that day.

The next morning we left at about the same time and took a packhorse with us - just in case. We had our lunches and a two-way radio so we could keep in touch with the outside world. Noon came and it was time for lunch. I noticed that it seemed Joe preferred to stand while eating rather than to share the log the other fellow and I occupied.

One thing that really chilled Joe about horses was their tendency to walk on the outside edge of a trail that led around a sidehill, above a slide or along a washout. He wondered why they didn't walk on the INSIDE edge? I don't know the answer either.

The day before season there were a lot of hunters in the area we were patrolling; so we started checking camps, letting everyone know that we were in the area. Then, on opening morning we were on our horses, off and runnin' at five bells. When we topped out on the Flat Tops we headed west towards Johnson Park and found where a dozen or so elk had crossed the main trail going south. These tracks had been made sometime around noon the day before and, seeing blood in their trail, it was evident that one of the elk had been wounded. We trailed this little bunch until they entered the heavy timber. The wounded animal was keeping up with the main herd so it apparently wasn't hurt badly.

From here on for the rest of the day we tried to obtain any information on pre-season hunting. One hunter said that he had heard some shooting the day before, but there was no way to find the guilty party.

As was our daily custom, we called Meeker on the two-way and were informed that we should return to civilization tomorrow. I was being called back to patrol a ranch area where there were reports of excessive spotlight hunting. So, we worked our way back to South Fork with plans to pull out for Meeker in the morning. I don't think Joe regretted that too much. He really took a beating from the long days in the saddle, but without a whimper. He was a heck of a good guy to have along, and with time I thought he'd get toughened into riding.

Although we didn't make any cases on this trip, we did contact a great number of hunters, so they were aware of our presence. As a consequence I feel that we discouraged a lot of the early hunting and other violations which might have occurred otherwise.

Chapter Twenty-Seven

One fall while patrolling the highways after dark I was headed south from Meeker. There were quite a few reports of spotlight hunting, and since this was the last week-end of the season it was apt to be a period of particular temptation to those "last minute" hunters.

Just a few miles from the junction of 789/13 and 64 I found an older station wagon parked along the highway. No lights. Instantly this looked suspicious. It was either a breakdown or, someone was "in pursuit".

At that time Highway 789 was closed area for a distance of one half mile on either side of the center line of the road.

I turned my spotlight on the auto and to the area

beyond, but didn't see anyone. I got out of my unit and with my flashlight started looking for empty rifle cases. I could see a rifle in the front seat and, then, one case lying behind the left front wheel. This case was not mashed by the wheel; so it had to have been fired after the auto stopped. All together I found four fresh-fired cases.

I started looking for man tracks, and soon found them on the shoulder of the road. It had rained a little just before dark, and these tracks had been made after the rain. I followed the tracks out to a deep wash about 125 yards from the highway. Then, when I shined my light down into the wash it exposed a slight-built man, and two fawn deer beside the creek that flowed down the wash.

As soon as he was aware that I had found him he stood up and shouted to me, asking if I would give him a hand in getting his deer out of the wash. I assured him that I would; but first he would have to gut them. I announced who I was, and held the light while he cleaned the deer.

When I asked him WHY he shot the deer - two fawns, which were illegal - in a closed area - after dark - with artificial light - from a public road, he said that, really, he'd shot the deer BEFORE dark. So? That would hardly solve all of his other problems.

He tried to tell me that he had been off the road when he shot the deer. When I showed him the empty cases, still lying on the oiled highway, BACK of his front wheel that still didn't make much of an impression - until I pointed out that they were 8mm cases, and the rifle in his car was a Mauser 8mm.

Finally, it was clear to him that all of his alibis were to no avail, and so he admitted his guilt. He implored me, though, that there were good and logical reasons for his actions.

He said that he was "on his uppers"; he'd wanted to try to get some meat for his family; he had borrowed a car and a gun from his boss; he'd scrounged up enough money to buy a deer license, and had taken off two days from work - all in hopes of filling the larder - and this was THE last day he could hunt; he HAD to be back to work tomorrow morning, or he'd "be canned". So, being desperate, he'd seen the two fawns on the road and decided that this was his last opportunity. And, now, here he was, about to be handed a summons!

We loaded the two fawns in my pickup and headed for Meeker. When I told him he'd have to go to court he almost fainted. I assured him that I would make every effort to have the trial that night so he could still make it back home in time to go to work the next day.

Upon our arrival in Meeker he parked in front of the courthouse as I had instructed and I went to get a Justice of the Peace to hear the case. When the J. P. agreed to hold court that night under the circumstances which I'd explained to him, I went out to tell the fellow that it was all set; we'd hold court just as soon as the Justice of the Peace arrived.

As I approached his car to tell him this I found him sitting in the driver's seat, holding a small, opened can of "Beanie-Weenies" on the steering wheel, picking bites out with his pocket knife, and tears were streaming down his face. That really got to me.

"Damn!" I thought, "WHY did he decide to shoot two little fawns, on the highway, in a restricted area? Now he's really in for it.

Of course, he didn't have any money to pay his fine. (He said that he only had enough money to buy gas to get home.) So, he was allowed to call his boss, and after so much negotiating between the violator, his boss, the Justice of the Peace and me, it was agreed that the boss would guarantee to send payment of the fine which would, in turn, be assessed against the fellow's wages.

There ARE some down-sides to law enforcement!

Chapter Twenty-Eight

One evening in March of 1981, my phone rang and upon answering it the voice on the other end was that of my nephew in Salmon, Idaho. He led off with the greeting, "How would you like to hunt bighorn sheep in Idaho this fall?" I answered, "OH, BOY! Any time I wouldn't like to hunt sheep ANYwhere will be a cold day in hell!"

Bill (coincidentally, his name is "Bill Goosman" also) was transferred to Salmon a little over a year before. At that time he was a range and recreation officer with the U.S. Forest Service.

During our conversation he informed me that the Idaho Game Department had adopted a new regulation pertaining to the application for a sheep permit. First, a hunter had to buy a hunting license at the cost of $60.50; then make application for a bighorn permit. If you weren't lucky enough to have your name drawn for a permit you would just lose the price of the license.

He said that if I wanted to gamble the cost of the hunting license he thought there would be an excellent chance of being drawn. And, if drawn, there would be a better than 50-50 chance of getting a shot at a good ram. We figured that this gamble on the cost of the hunting license would wash out a number of would-be applicants, thereby increasing my chances of being drawn for a permit.

I immediately followed up this conversation with an "O.K." for Bill to purchase a hunting license for me. As soon as I received the necessary form from him I sent in my application for the bighorn permit.

Along in August one day when I picked up my mail there was an envelope from the Idaho Game Department. You guessed it! I had been drawn for a bighorn permit for that fall in the Middle Fork of the Salmon River area.

I had already received a permit to hunt antelope in Wyoming that same fall, and had made plans with a hunting companion to be on deck for that hunt on opening day which was September 12th. As a result, when I received the bighorn permit I called Bill to inform him of my success, and explained that because of the prior commitment for antelope hunting I would not be able to leave for the Idaho sheep hunt until September 24th.

I departed my home in Meeker early that morning and arrived in Salmon on the evening of the 25th. The final preparations were made for our flight the next morning when we would leave for Cal Stoddard's base camp at Storm Meadows.

As the pilot of the Cessna 210 banked his heavily loaded plane towards the pass in the high range of mountains west of Salmon a dense fog was racing towards the pass and obscuring the peaks. When we were almost to the pass and the heaviest of the fog, the plane's radio cut in on the drone of the engine advising of a very heavy front just beyond the pass. Upon receiving that information the pilot asked us if we wanted to turn back - or - "test" the storm ahead of us. Without any hesitation at all both Bill and I agreed, "Head 'er back, and wait a while for the storm to clear out."

About an hour later we tried it again and this time we made it through all right, but had to land at a private lodge about ten minutes short of Storm Meadows.

Bill had arranged with the outfitter, Cal, to pack us into our proposed camp some twenty-four miles further on, to the Middle Fork of the Salmon. After another wait of close to an hour at the private lodge we made a run at it again. This time we reached the dirt strip at Storm Meadows. As we taxied to a stop at the loading area we were met by Cal and some of his crew.

As soon as our gear was unloaded the pilot said, "Good huntin', guys! I'm gettin' the hell outa' here before the soup moves in." As he made the turn at the end of the runway he threw the coal on and the 210 came roaring down the strip by us. Soon he was a mere speck against the storm clouds, heading for the pass.

This is a heavily timbered, mountainous country. The Middle Fork of the Salmon River is well known for its remote, rough terrain. Also, this area is an excellent producer of big bull elk. Some parts of it have good bighorn sheep hunting, too. During the flight, despite the fog and the snow storm, I had an opportunity to observe just how heavily timbered this country is. There are no roads into this area, just horseback trails. This is a big, clean, beautiful country - unspoiled by the modern day hurrah of civilization.

After lunch Cal wanted to check a couple of his elk camps and suggested that Bill and I ride along as we wouldn't pack out to our camp until the next day. When the horses were brought in I noticed that there were quite a number of mules along with the horses. Since this is a very rocky country with hard ground a lot of mules are used as pack animals. In British Columbia and the Yukon Territory where it is very boggy mules are not used due to their small feet which tend to cause the animals to "bog down" much easier than horses which have bigger hoofs.

We dropped off some supplies and looked over a couple of nice elk heads at one camp. Then we checked the other camp and learned that one of the hunters had shot a good six-point bull the evening before; however, it hadn't been packed in yet.

The next morning, after a hearty breakfast, we packed up our outfit, ready to head for our intended hunting camp, located at an old fire station lookout.

We no sooner rode out of the saddling area than one of the mules, loaded with bed rolls, eggs, etc., and tailed to another mule, bowed its head and bucked until it snapped the lead rope. By this time the string of four pack mules were either bucking or running through the timber, shedding our gear and provisions as they went! They were finally rounded up, vehemently threatened, repacked and - we were on our way again.

As this was in Bill's district he had a pretty good idea of the drainages where we were likely to find the bighorns. We rode steady all day, not even stopping for lunch; we just ate our sandwiches as we rode, and arrived at our destination only minutes ahead of a snowstorm. Camp was made in an old shed instead of pitching the 10 x 12 wall tent I'd taken along.

A tarp was hung over the opening to serve as a "door". The saddle horses and pack mules were hobbled or picketed while supper was cooked and other camp chores were completed. Before hitting the sack plans were made for tomorrow. Cal would return to Storm Meadows headquarters, leaving two saddle horses and two pack mules for Bill and me. He was to return for us in eight days unless I got my ram before the last day. If I did, one of us would ride out to his main camp to report the successful hunt and return with Cal and the pack string to pack us out.

The next morning dawned clear with the promise of a beautiful day. After Cal was saddled up and on his way back to his base camp, Bill and I headed for a drainage that connected with the Salmon River, some four or five miles from our camp. This was the first time I'd ever hunted DOWNHILL for bighorn sheep!

By 10:30 a.m. we had ridden back up on a ridge where Bill wanted to leave the horses and continue by foot to the high point of the ridge. Earlier in the summer Bill had seen sheep on the mountainside across the canyon from this point.

We searched and researched the ledges, side canyons and grassy mountainside meadows with our binoculars. All we were able to locate were eleven head of ewes and lambs. By 3:00 o'clock we decided to give it up and work our way back to camp. We didn't find any more sheep although we glassed all likely "sheepy"-looking mountains.

That night the sky was clear with millions of stars shining and a cold breeze blowing across the fire lookout station where we were camped chilled the air considerably.

The next morning while I cooked breakfast of hot-cakes, bacon and eggs, Bill got the horses ready. After eating we rode off the top of the mountain where our camp was. We could see the Middle Fork of the Salmon far below us, shining like a silver ribbon threading its way through the vast mountain range.

After a couple of miles by saddle horse we picket-ed the horses in a little meadow with lush grass for them to feed on until we returned. From here we worked our way on down the ridge. We soon located a herd of twenty-one ewes and lambs feeding in one of the many mountainside meadows. They were beyond the end of the ridge we were on, and to the right, only about a mile from the river. We worked to a good observation point where we had lunch.

Soon after resuming glassing Bill said, "I've got four more sheep spotted and I think they're rams." I took a look where he pointed using my 10 x 40 binoc-ulars. I could definitely see horns, but they were not too clear. I set up my spotting scope and zoomed it up to 35-power. This brought the rams up to where we could study them well. After several minutes of glassing them I rolled away from the scope so Bill could look and I could rest my eyes. He no sooner took his place behind the scope than he said, "Hey! I just saw a ram turn his head and the horn I could see looked like a keeper!"

The rams were all bedded down except for one

half-curl. As we watched, this small fry fed out into a clearing and after so much pawing of the ground - apparently to rearrange the rocks - he lay down. After getting settled he was facing our ridge with a clear view of anything that moved. The other three rams remained bedded down in some rocks. Two of the three were in good view. One looked to be slightly over a three-quarter curl, and the other was a full curl, unbroomed, and with thin horns. The fourth ram was out of sight except when he would turn his head. The few times that he did turn would give us a chance to see that the right horn, at least, was heavy all the way out, as well as being heavily broomed; and - it was a full curl.

After carefully studying the situation I decided that the best route for a stalk of the rams was down the side of the ridge which was partially open to the view of the ewes, instead of in view of the little ram which was bedded down in the clearing on the left side of "our" ridge.

Since the stalk had to be made across this open space which would no doubt be watched by the ewes, I suggested that Bill stay put - with the spotting scope - and keep an eye on all of the sheep. Meanwhile, I began the stalk.

I kept a constant watch on the ewes and lambs to see if they were aware of my descent down the side of the ridge from the high point where Bill remained. About mid-way down I was reminded of a joke I had heard one time. It went like this: An optimistic guy bet one of his friends that he could jump off a twenty-story building and land okay. As he passed the tenth floor he said, "So far so good!"

I had picked a clump of tall yellow pines down

the ridge further as being even with the three bedded rams. If I could reach these trees I should be able to inspect the rams and would be about 300 yards away. I'd prefer to be closer, but a 300-yard shot with my 7mm Model 70 Winchester Magnum is a fairly easy shot at a standing ram or one lying down where I can see all of him broadside.

I reached the trees after a good two and a half hours. When I eased up to where I could see the rocks that the rams were supposed to be bedded down on, the rocks were there all right but - no rams! I knew that the rams could very well have worked in my direction when they started out to feed after getting up. I crawled up behind one of the big pines and very slowly stood up. This enabled me to look over the crest of the ridge, and instantly I saw the rams, including the little half-curl - feeding among some brush to the left of where I'd last seen them bedded down.

The old heavy-horned ram stood out like a sore thumb. As I was deciding my next move the big ram with the broomed horns and the lighter-horned full-curl came face to face. The lighter-horned ram reared up as if to take a punch at the old ram. Upon seeing this threat the old ram bowed his neck and tipped his horns out in the position to take the forthcoming slam from the younger ram. This effort turned out to be a false pass at the big ram; but at the same time I took advantage of the four rams being off guard. I slipped in behind another pine a good ten yards closer; this would give me a commanding view of the side of the mountain they were on.

As I eased the 7mm Mag. around the side of the pine all four of the rams moved into single file and started walking to my left. The distance I guessed at about 275 yards. As the cross hairs of the 4X Redfield settled just back of center of the ram's shoulder I squeezed the trigger. At the blast of the rifle the old ram hit the dirt as if the rug had suddenly been jerked out from under him. The payload of this shot was my favorite - a 154 grain Hornady ahead of 66 grains of 4831. This load works well in my gun, however each shooter should use his own discretion concerning any hand load. This shot made my 24th one-shot kill of big game animals with this rifle.

I'm a great believer in the slogan, "Practice Makes Perfect". I shoot up boxes of hand loads during the period from one hunting season to the next. Most of my shooting is done at estimated yardage from the off-hand, sitting and kneeling positions.

As the old ram hit the ground he was in ram heaven. I sized up the scene, looked at my watch and saw that it was 3:00 p.m. The three other rams didn't leave until I was about eighty yards from them. I had an excellent chance to study them, especially the full curl one. He had a good four inches longer horns than the old ram had; but they were much slimmer. The annual rings on my ram's horns indicated that he was twelve years old. There was a small chunk knocked out of the top of each horn, apparently due to fighting.

Bill joined me; he had been able to watch the whole drama unfold before him from his lofty lookout up on the ridge above. We took pictures, skinned out the cape up to the ram's head and hung the meat in a pine tree to be packed out the next day.

At this point Bill took off to go back after the horses and I would start up for the ridge. By dusk I had topped out on the first ridge and was satisfied that Bill had reached the horses, but figured that it was too late for him to attempt getting back to me before dark. We had agreed that if this happened he would go on back to camp and would return for me in the morning.

I found a good windbreak behind a huge rock, dragged up a supply of firewood, and made a pad out of pine boughs to rest on. After eating a chunk of backstrap broiled over the embers I leaned back against the rock and admired the trophy ram head that seemed to dance in the shadows from the flickering flames of the fire.

As night closed in over the mountains the stars twinkled in the cloudless sky. I doubt if there was a more contented man anywhere in the world than I was.

Chapter Twenty-Nine

One fall there was a decision made between the Cattlemen's Association and the Game Department. The Cattlemen would hire men who would be deputized by the sheriff to work with game wardens who had districts in the cattle ranching areas. This would include "Open Range", accessible to big game hunters.

The plan was devised in hopes of apprehending any cattle rustlers who might be operating in the area. There was the possibility that if a game warden was checking a hunter for big game he might uncover a beef that had been rustled.

Jim Findlay, a local man, was chosen to ride with me. I'd known this fellow for years and we got along well. The third day that Jim worked with me we ate an early supper and then went on patrol up Flag Creek. About three miles from town we met a car headed back to town. We immediately recognized the outfit; it belonged to a man who had a long history of game violations.

The car passed us going rather slowly, and we noted all of the occupants. We also saw rifles in the car above the back seat. At this point I whipped my pickup around and soon overtook them.

It really looked like we'd hit "pay dirt". I told Jim to let me do the talking and for him to cover my back. We knew that the driver was a dangerous man; he had proven so in the past.

I turned on my red lights as we caught up with them. I knew that we had to act quickly, not giving them time to think matters out. As they stopped I pulled ahead of them about eight or ten feet. I said to Jim, "Keep your eyes open; this COULD get sticky!"

I stepped up to the car and addressed the driver by name. Then I asked if his trunk was locked. In a slurred voice he muttered, "'Tain't locked - an' I s'pose you wanna' look in ut." Yes, I did, and walked around to the back of the car, quickly jerking the lid open. No meat! But, there lying on some meat sacks was a meat saw, a cleaver and two or three butcher knives. About this time - ANOTHER "lid" blew off!!

The doors popped open and the occupants boiled out - surrounding me pronto. Everyone was trying to talk at the same time. It was quite evident that the driver and one other man had been doing a little drinking. I advised them that they were lucky this time; but if they didn't get back in their car and get headed out of there I was going to call the sheriff on my two-way radio and the driver would probably end up with a room in the city jug for the night.

At this stage of matters the driver, who was the farthest from me, barked, "I'll get a gun and shoot you, you son-of-a-bitch!" And he started toward the car. As he opened the right rear door I hollered at him to forget it. I warned him that if he pulled a gun on me it would be the last one he'd ever pick up. As I made this statement I pushed my jacket back and hooked my thumb in my belt just ahead of my holstered .357 Magnum. The guy standing next to me said, "I think you really mean that, Bill." Without waiting for my reply he made a few long strides and grabbed the driver around the middle just as the driver was backing out of the car with a .270 Winchester in his hands.

The fellow who had grabbed the driver shook him so hard that he dropped the rifle, then this man snatched up the gun and, with the muzzle pointing at the ground, ran over and handed it to me.

Knowing the operation of a Model 70 Winchester very well, I pushed the release button and pulled the bolt out of the rifle. That rendered the gun harmless and this action was enough to jar the driver back to reality. He started crying.

I wouldn't have backed down one bit, even if the rifle hadn't been shaken loose from the threatener. To do so would have meant that I might as well "Pack my suitcase and move out".

After things quieted down and we were headed on up Flag Creek, Jim drew a deep breath and remarked, "WHEEE-YOOO!!! Bill, I wouldn't have your job for $5,000.00 a month!" I'll agree with him; sometimes it was a thankless job; but it was necessary, and - it was my choice.

The next day an F.B.I. agent whom I knew saw me

at the post office. He had heard about the incident of the night before and gave me a warning, "Don't take any crap off of THAT guy, Bill; he's paid for!"

Later that same day my "adversary" came to me and apologized! But, he added a caveat; he cautioned me to never let him get the upper hand because when he was drinking he might do anything. It was a point well taken!

Chapter Thirty

Sometime after the first of February I would make a trip up the South Fork of White River to its confluence with Patterson Creek to check on conditions of the elk that wintered in the South Fork Canyon. This usually took about two days depending on snow conditions as well as other factors.

Since the trip was made on snowshoes travel would really slow down if the snow was loose or sticky. The plan was to stay at my cabin at the mouth of Lost Solar Creek. It was always stocked and I used it for my base on any trips in this area. The only trouble was that it was on the opposite side of the river from the trail leading up-country.

In the summer I was usually on horseback which

took care of crossing the river. The horse did the wading while I sat high and dry in the saddle. Wintertime crossings over to the cabin posed a different situation as it was necessary to find some place where the water was frozen completely across the river; sometimes these places were hard to find. The South Fork, like many other high country streams, flows rather fast, which keeps the water from entirely freezing over.

One winter when this annual trip came up a Game and Fish Department biologist living in Meeker wanted to go along. He was on a big game study at the time and this trip would put him into part of the elk wintering range. Perhaps he could gather some dope for his report.

By the time we arrived at the South Fork campground it was the middle of the afternoon and the snow was a little sticky. We both had about thirty-five pound packs which wasn't too bad, but they did cause us to sink into the snow a bit deeper.

When we arrived at the spot on the trail which was across from my cabin it was just starting to get dusk. The trail that leads across the river to the cabin is close to a pole fence where the water was open for a distance of perhaps six or seven feet through the middle of the river.

Up to this point we hadn't found a place that was completely frozen over enabling us to cross without wading in the frigid water. With darkness coming on I decided that we could take three or four poles off the fence and span the open water; then we would soon be over to the cabin.

I told Don what I was thinking and he agreed. I gathered that he was tired of snowshoeing by this time anyway, and the quicker we were on our way across to the cabin the better.

We took a couple of the poles off the fence, carried them over to the narrowest open water, and while Don went back for another pole I removed my snowshoes and pack, then jumped down onto the snow-covered ice. I grabbed a pole and stood it up on end in the snow on the ice. Holding the pole this way I let it fall, spanning the open water. So far this was working as planned.

As I slid the other pole off the bank I noticed Don coming with a third pole. I stood my second pole up on end and gave it a solid jab into the snow to seat it against the first pole. When I did this it was just enough force to break off the ice I was standing on - and I plunged into about three and a half feet of icy river water - belly down!

I came up clawin' for the bank and as soon as I could get my breath I hollered at Don to grab one of my snowshoes holding it out for me to use as an assist to get out of the water. Then, while he was pursuing the snowshoe I grabbed onto a willow that was nearby and was already climbing up onto the bank when I looked around to see what had happened to Don.

He was in the process of getting untangled from one of my shoes which he'd caught in his! For an instant the image reminded me of a three-legged dog paying tribute to a fireplug!

I shouted, "Grab your pack and we'll wade across to the cabin!" He commented, though, that he really didn't want to get wet and wondered if there was another cabin on THIS side of the river that we could use.

It so happened that a good friend of mine had a cabin about a mile further on upstream. I mentioned this to him and told him that it would take close to another hour to make it with the snow conditions as they were. When he elected to try for it I didn't argue. I had to get moving or freeze!

We grabbed our packs, buckled on our webs and headed out "muy pronto"! By that time my clothes had frozen, shutting out the cold air, but my teeth sounded like they would rattle right out of my head.

About an hour later we had a fire going in my friend's cabin and I started thawing out. Don wound up packing all the water and wood as I didn't get very far away from the stove.

The following day was spent checking elk in the South Fork Canyon. We stayed at the cabin that night, and then snowshoed out the next day.

In the process of all this I wondered if I'd found a new cure for the common cold. I didn't even catch one from the dunkin' in the river!

Chapter Thirty-One

A game warden's duties were varied; some were routine and performed on a daily basis. Others were unique and experienced only on rare occasions. Following is an example of the latter.

One fall just before hunting season opened the Director of the Department informed my district supervisor that he and two of the Department Commissioners and a doctor friend would be in Meeker and if I was going to patrol the high country on horseback they would like to ride along for three or four days. They wanted to see first hand what took place and get some ideas of hunter density as well as elk conditions on the Flat Tops.

This would be primarily elk hunting country,

although there were a few big buck mule deer that called the Flat Tops home until being driven out to the lower country by snow. Very few hunters ever planned any serious deer hunting up there, however.

Two days before season opened the Director, the two Commissioners and the doctor, and I, headed up South Fork from the campground. I had two pack horses to haul the food, equipment and their personal duffel. The plan was to house the group in my cabin at the mouth of Lost Solar Creek. Located about six miles above the campground it was somewhat centralized in the area we planned to cover.

We had almost reached the cabin when down the trail came a horsebacker at a full gallop, as if he was being chased by the devil himself. When he neared us he steered out of the trail and started "sawing" on the reins in a frenzied effort to stop his horse.

Finally he paused, and I asked him where he was going in such a hurry. He tried to tell us, all too fast, stumbling over his words as they tumbled forth so rapidly that we couldn't understand much of what he was trying to say. It seemed as though someone was dying. I urged him to slow down; maybe we could help him. My first thought was that perhaps he had shot another hunter. When I asked him if that was what happened he said, "No, but is there a doctor in your group? I NEED a doctor!" Yes, there was a doctor in our group!

Again, asking him what had happened he explained that his partner was in a diabetic coma, and was dying; he needed a doctor, QUICK!

We learned that there were only the two of them in the party and that they were camped up on top of Bloomfield Bench close to a 150-foot drop-off of the cliff. This bench is high above the South Fork River and just north of the property I owned. It runs around the mountain for probably a mile and is where cattle summered in the early days. As the story was told to me, the bench got its name as a direct result of a roundup one fall. It seems that a bronc started bucking out at the edge of the cliff and fell over the rim, with a cowboy named Bloomfield still in the saddle.

The hunter pointed out where their camp was, and said that his partner was in a sleeping bag. I suggested that he get back up there and watch the sick man so he didn't flounder around and roll off the cliff. The doctor would accompany him. The rest of us would go on to my cabin and unload the pack horses; then we would arrive at his camp as soon as possible.

Kit, my main pack horse, was a big strong animal and she never failed to pack anything that I could load on her. So, I would take her. After reaching the cabin and unloading we high-tailed it up the steep climb to the hunters' camp, leading Kit.

When we reached the camp we soon learned that the man was in very bad shape. The doctor had done what he could for him, but told us that the only chance the fellow had was to get him to the hospital in Meeker, as soon as possible.

Getting him down to an automobile at the campground looked like a hopeless task; and then there would be the continuing journey from the campground on into Meeker. But, we had to try, by any and all means.

The sick man was absolutely helpless, of course; so he couldn't sit in a saddle. And, I sure couldn't lay him across a pack saddle and lash him down. We'd have to do something else.

The only thing I could think of was to make a stretcher out of aspen poles, lay him on it, and then we would sling the stretcher between my pack horse and one of the hunters' horses. It would be a tandem pack and, not knowing whether Kit and the other horse would work together, we'd just have to hope for the best.

We built the stretcher and, putting Kit in the lead and the other horse in the back we lashed the fore ends of the contraption to Kit's pack saddle and the aft ends to the saddle on the other horse. I then mounted my horse and, taking a dally around the saddle horn, I started out to test the set-up before we loaded the patient on board. Everything looked good for a few steps; then the horses decided that they'd had enough of this circus and all hell broke loose! Both horses started bucking and when the dust settled we didn't have much of our stretcher left.

Well, let's see; how about a travois? No, that wouldn't work due to the nature of the terrain we'd be traveling, along a sidehill trail. We really would have a wreck if we decided to do that! So, I could see right then that the only way to get the man out would be the stretcher, tie him onto it in his sleeping bag and, with a man on each end of the two stretcher poles, head off the mountain. The doctor had said that the man wouldn't last until morning; so our only alternative was to start packing.

With the stretcher patched up, four of us and the doctor headed out with our patient. Other hunters had arrived on the scene; so we asked one of them to go to the campground and call for an ambulance.

Nearly four and a half hours later, well after dark, we arrived at the campground. We had enlisted the help of other hunters along the way, and two of them had led our horses down to the campground for us, saving us a six-mile hike back to the cabin.

The ambulance was waiting for us. Unfortunately it was too late. The man had succumbed just a short distance before reaching the campground.

Chapter Thirty-Two

This morning dawned with hopes that it would be a better day than yesterday had been. The Department Director, two of the Game Commissioners, a doctor and I had joined a hunter to bring his seriously ill partner from Bloomfield Bench down to the South Fork campground. Our efforts had been in vain for the patient, however, as he did not survive. We looked forward to this new day as one free of any such ordeals.

After breakfast we made a patrol up Solar Creek and into Park Creek. Then we headed down Park Creek to South Fork and back to my cabin. On the way out of Park Creek and about a mile before we reached the river we heard a rifle shot south of the river and up on the mountain above the South Fork

Canyon. We heard the report of the rifle and immediately thereafter we heard the "ker-thunk" of a bullet hitting meat. I looked at the Director and said, "Well, Boss, there is my work lined up for tomorrow. That bullet hit meat and I intend to try to find it tomorrow."

It was too late in the day to try to look for it then. It would take at least an hour to climb out of South Fork to the top of the mountain and it would be dark by then. Tomorrow would be the opening day of season, so if I could find a hunter with a cold, stiff elk in the morning I would have my man.

The next morning, opening day, I was on my way to investigate the shot we had heard yesterday evening. I had to work up river to an elk trail that I knew of which led to the top of the mountain. It would be a steep climb even with a good horse like mine. At that time I weighed about 180; my saddle probably another 35 to 40 pounds; rifle and saddle bags another 10 pounds. So, my horse would have a good load.

It took me a little over an hour to climb out onto the top. I rested my horse quite often and each time I would dismount, giving my horse all the chance possible to rest. At the same time I would glass the rim and what I could see of the mountain side.

On my first rest stop I located three people out on some rocks up on the rim. One man was watching me through the scope on a rifle while the other two were using binoculars. They were near the trail where it topped out. Each time I stopped I would check them with my 10-power binoculars. Each time they were watching me, too.

When I topped out I could see that they were

camped just back of the rim and they had a jeep. From where they were camped it was only about a quarter of a mile to the road that leads from Hiner Spring to the top of Blair Mountain; therefore, they didn't need any horses. Miles of this top south of the South Fork River could be hunted by jeep or pickup.

I rode over to them and dismounted, walked over and sat down on a convenient log. One of the men said, "That was quite a ride up outa' there; we watched you all the way." I replied that I knew it was, and that I also knew they were watching me, one of them using a scope on a rifle to do so. I looked at my watch and it was almost 9:00 a.m.

I noticed that the license plates on the jeep were from Garfield County, and there was a boy about ten to twelve years old in the group. When I was offered a cup of coffee I was aware that the guy with the rifle was really sizing me up. By then he had leaned the gun against a tree which put me at some ease.

I was wearing riding boots, chaps, a wool jacket, western hat with a red ribbon around the crown, and a six-shooter on my belt. There was a rifle in the scabbard on my saddle.

The guy who had been looking me over suddenly asked, "Just who are you anyway?" He continued, "We've been watching you all the way up and I don't think you're just another hunter because you have a lot of consideration for your horse. Besides that you are constantly watching everything around you, including us. I'd say you're a sheriff, or some law man looking for someone - maybe you're a game warden!"

"You're right. Yes, I'm Bill Goosman, the game warden from Meeker and I AM looking for someone.

Someone who shot a deer or an elk yesterday evening about an hour before dark." I told them about hearing the shot, and knowing that the bullet hit a animal.

One of the men said, "Yes, we heard the shot, too; but didn't know that it hit anything." The first guy spoke up then and said, "Yeah - the shot was about a half to a mile from here we guessed. It was east of here, and we don't like it either! We try to abide by the laws and it also messes up OUR hunting." In parting one added, "I hope you get the guy and if you need any help just let us know."

I thanked them for the coffee and their attitude towards hunters who "jump the gun" and don't wait until season opens. Then I mounted up and headed for a high ridge east of their camp. From this ridge I intended to really glass the surrounding country for any hunting activity. As I rode toward the ridge I thought to myself, "Boy, this is going to be like looking for the proverbial needle in a haystack."

I rode up onto the ridge between two clumps of pine trees and immediately saw a small column of smoke rising above the timber about 400 yards from me. As I watched this timber for a few minutes I was finally able to make out part of a vehicle in the edge of the pines.

Heading for that patch of timber I reached it to find a camp and the campfire causing the smoke. At first I didn't see anyone around, then I spotted a man hunkered down behind a log - watching me. "Good morning!" I greeted him. He just grunted in return and stood up. He was holding a long-bladed knife in his right hand and I could see blood on his left hand. I stepped off my horse and walked over to him. Behind the log and brush lay a bull elk with two points on each antler and no tag was evident on the animal.

As I stepped over the log I said, "Well, it looks like you connected on one." As he didn't answer me I then asked him if he had killed it close to this camp. Again he just looked at me; his face was pale - and - he was still hangin' onto the big knife. I thought to myself that I'd better bring this guy out of the trance he was in, so I told him who I was. That did the job all right, as he started denouncing his luck and telling me what he thought of "sneaky game wardens". I told him to "knock it off" and to do something with that big knife; either stick it in a log or put it in the scabbard on his belt. I didn't like him waving it around in front of me.

He jammed the knife down in an old log while I looked the elk over and felt of the meat on the hind quarters. It was cold; the eyes were sunken and most of the blood on the animal was dry. He had started to skin one hind leg and, of course, there the blood wasn't dry yet.

After the shock wore off of being caught "redhanded" he admitted shooting the elk the evening before; no doubt the results of the shot we'd heard.

I gave the man a summons for possession of an illegally killed bull elk, then used an indelible pen to make a circle around one antler. I told him just to leave it the way it was and that I'd be back in a little while with a vehicle to pick it up, and to be darned sure he stayed in camp. At the same time I relieved him of his hunting license, and then I rode back to the camp where the jeep was. The only road that he could get out of the area on was the one that ran past the other hunters' camp that was out on the rim.

Also, the violator had said that his partner was out hunting and wouldn't be back until around noon. So I felt sure things were under control while I went for a vehicle.

Arriving back at the first camp I told them what I'd found and asked them if I could borrow their jeep to get the elk out. The guys were happy to hear that I'd found the illegal hunter and the elk. The owner of the jeep said, "Mister, I don't want to loan the jeep; but I'll drive it anywhere you ask me to, and we'll go along and help." When we left their camp there were the three men, the boy and I in the jeep. We drove over to the other camp and, sure enough, the hunter was still there, as was the elk. We loaded the bull onto the jeep and hauled it back to their camp. As we hung it in the shade I placed a seizure tag on it just in case another game warden would come by. I told them that I'd be up sometime toward evening the next day to get it. I'd have to ride out to my pickup at the South Fork campground, leave my horse there, then drive down to Buford and on up the Buford-Newcastle road to Hiner Spring, then east on the Blair Mountain road to the camp where I had left the elk. From there I would have to deliver the elk to the locker plant in Meeker, return to the South Fork campground, get my horse and ride back to the cabin.

The Director and the Commissioners, and the doctor, were waiting to hear my story of the day's events, and thought I'd hit a good lick. One of the Commissioners commented, though, that when I left that morning he had thought I was going on a "wild goose chase". I told him that a lot of times it turned out that way, but now and then one worked out in the warden's favor. I asked them if they would want to accompany me the next day. "No thanks, Bill," was one's reply, "You could get a guy shot."

The next morning I saddled up and headed for the campground. I made my circle to pick up the elk, deliver it to the locker plant, and return to the campground where my four-legged transportation awaited me. Just after dark I arrived back at my cabin.

The summoned hunter went to court in Meeker and was fined $250.00 plus costs.

Chapter Thirty-Three

Fred LeTendre, my guide, drained the last swallow from his coffee cup and stood up from the breakfast table, while taking a deep drag on his ever-present cigarette. He stepped to the tent flap and looked out at the start of a new day on the Nisling River in the Yukon Territory. Without turning around he exclaimed over his shoulder, "I think we'll take a pack horse along today, just in case something needs hauled outa' the bush." Knowing Fred, his comment put that way didn't leave much doubt in my mind as to the outcome of the day.

This was the second stage of a three-week mixed bag hunt I made in the fall of 1972. Two days ago I had shot a very nice Dall ram downstream from camp. Yesterday was used to finish taking care of the cape and horns, getting out the sheep meat that had been hung at the site of the kill, and other odd jobs.

Starting this morning the main item on the agenda was a grizzly, and a moose second. It was still some time off until the moose and caribou would shed the velvet from their antlers; so we were really looking for the grizzly more than moose right now.

All morning and until noon we stuck to the ridges and high ground so we could glass down into the valleys from above them. So far we had ridden and glassed mile after mile of unspoiled, wild beautiful mountains and valleys. Here the solitude and vastness of this magnificent country sets a man's mind at ease with the world. A mile or two across the main river drainage I could see a golden eagle circling the top of a high mountain. Beyond this point I could see seven head of Dall sheep feeding near a saddle between two peaks. Even with my 10 x 40 binoculars I couldn't tell much about them other than it looked like they were small rams.

By noon we hadn't spotted any grizzly or moose; so we picked a high point on which to eat lunch and glass the surrounding country. While munching our sandwiches I spotted two black animals that at first I thought to be black bear. These two spots which were about two miles off were in a patch of blueberry bushes. We trained the spotting scope on them and were quite surprised to see two black wolves eating berries like a bear would. This was the first time that either Fred or I had seen wolves eating blueberries!

Off and on while eating lunch and glassing the surrounding country we'd take a look at the wolves. When we cinched up our saddles and pulled out, the wolves were still gorging themselves in the berry patch.

Shortly after leaving the high knob where we ate lunch we jumped a bull moose out of a draw choked with willows. Since we didn't get a good look at the antlers we crashed the horses through the brush to the hillside opposite from where the moose was headed. When he cleared the brush across the valley from me I was all ready to take him if he was what I wanted. As he trotted up the hill above the brush about two hundred yards away we could see that he was only average; so, let him go.

A bull moose, no matter what size his antlers are, is a striking animal and those long legs can cover ground quickly. After he disappeared over the ridge we retrieved our pack horse and continued the hunt.

About the middle of the afternoon we hadn't seen any more game, so headed our ponies toward camp. After slabbing a mountain we spotted a moose about 450 yards across a valley in some scattered timber and brush. A quick look through the glasses proved him to be over average size. We eased the horses back out of sight and tied up.

After the route was chosen for the stalk we started working in on the bull. By now we had decided he would fill the bill. Although his antlers were still in the velvet they were huge and the points were pretty well formed and should peel out of the velvet in good shape.

We were coming up on the bull's left side; he was standing between two pine trees and looked as solid as a granite boulder. When we had cut the distance down to about two hundred fifty yards we found that to go any further would put us down in heavy brush and out of sight of the bull. The shot would have to be made from here.

I settled in my favorite sitting position with the Winchester over my left knee. When I leveled the cross hairs on "Old Banjo Nose", just back of the left shoulder I couldn't help but wonder what would happen when I dumped the Nosler into his oversized boiler room!

Fred was kneeling just back of me to observe the results which were to follow. As the "hairs" in the scope settled I touched off the Magnum. To the amazement of both Fred and me the bull showed no sign whatever that he had been shot at - let alone hit!

I slipped another round into the chamber, lined up the scope on the same spot and tightened up on the trigger. At the blast of the 7mm there was absolutely NO sign of a hit! Then, I bolted a THIRD round into the chamber and asked, over my shoulder to Fred, "What in the hell is holding that big rascal up?" Fred just grunted.

At this time I held for a base of the neck shot and squeezed 'er off. As the Magnum recoiled I saw the huge bull hit the ground as if lightening had struck him. We stayed put for a few minutes just in case the old boy wasn't as "finished" as he appeared to be.

As we continued to watch the fallen bull, Fred explained, "A bull moose isn't too hard to kill; but it takes a little while for all of those big nerves and muscles to get the message that it's all over."

As I walked over to where the bull lay Fred went back for the horses. Upon checking him we found that the two rib shots were about three inches apart, right back of the left shoulder, and the third shot had broken the neck, as planned. The tape showed sixty-two inches as the greatest spread.

We also measured the height of this animal from

the heel of his front foot to the top of the shoulder. We didn't stretch the foreleg, but let it assume the position as much as possible as if he were alive. The tape showed seven feet four inches. On top of this figure is most of the antler height. When viewing a big bull traveling through stunted pines and brush it is a most impressive sight. Equally impressive is the size of these critters' noses. My first thought was if I had that snoot stuffed with twenty dollar bills I could make a good sheep hunt on it!

We took some pictures and caped out the head, then pulled the quarters up into a pine tree; they would be picked up tomorrow. Then we loaded the trophy head on the pack horse that Fred had thought we should bring along in case "something needs hauled out".

In camp that night we learned that both Dick and Flay had connected on rams and quite a bit of fresh grizzly sign had been seen. Everyone was in good spirits tonight, and a toast was made to the Yukon and its wildlife.

Tomorrow would be spent finishing the caping job on the moose and packing out the meat that we'd hung in the pine tree. During the process of cleaning up the moose trophy and packing out the meat Fred and I made plans to head into a "fly camp" tomorrow - for grizzly and caribou.

Chapter Thirty-Four

This morning when I woke up I started running plans through my mind for the up-coming hunting season. I planned to pack into my base camp at Lost Solar Creek and patrol the high country for two days before season opened and maybe the the first two days of the season, depending on how the hunt went. Then I would high-tail it back down to the civilized area and use the pickup to patrol with.

During breakfast the phone rang and upon my answering it it was Cleve, the boss. He had gotten some information on early hunting down on Piceance Creek and wanted me to drop everything and check this out. I did so that day with making one arrest. This was three days before season and tomorrow I would have to be in court at 10:00 a.m. After that I could round up things quickly and pull out for Lost Solar Creek.

About dark I arrived at my cabin. Up on a bench to the south of my place I could hear a coyote complaining to the quarter moon. I thought how peaceful it was up here. No automobiles running around, or electric lights shining...just the night sounds of nature. However, I was sure a change in the weather was coming. Several indications were apparent such as that coyote howling; I'd seen three porcupines up in trees, and there was a big ring around the moon.

The next morning, the day before opening day of season, I was in the saddle and headed up Lost Solar Creek before the sun came up. My plans were to travel up Lost Solar to the Flat Tops, then swing east to the headwaters of Park Creek and Doe Creek. From there I'd go back to Oyster Lake and hole up with an outfitter friend of mine who had his main elk camp situated near the lake; at least that is where he did have one for several years. I had my sleeping bag and a very light camp on Kit, my pack horse.

The farther up Lost Solar that I went the more snow was on the ground. It started snowing about noon and by the time I had reached the head of Park creek it was snowing pretty hard and sure looked like "No-Man's Land". I hadn't found a camp since I'd topped out at the head of Lost Solar Creek; so I decided to turn back west and hit Beard's camp at Oyster Lake. I arrived at this area about dark. I checked where the camp should be, but no sign of a camp could I find. At this point the snow was a good fourteen inches deep. There would be very little feed for my horses, except about ten pounds of oats I had in my pack. I thought this over for a minute or two, then decided to head back to my cabin down on the river. I figured that if I traveled steady I could make it by 10:00 or 11:00 p.m. if I headed down Bear Creek to Lost Solar, then on down it to South Fork. Sally, my saddle horse, knew the way even after dark; so about all I had to do was sit in the saddle and dream of a nice warm pickup to do my patrolling in.

Soon after I headed down Bear Creek I could smell smoke. I knew that said smoke was coming from a camp where a fella could get out of the saddle and up close to a warm fire; maybe even get a bite of warm food to eat. I had been riding almost steady for about thirteen hours and if I didn't stop at this camp I'd probably have another two and a half to three hours of riding before getting back to the cabin.

As I came closer to the camp I could hear horse bells and then I could make out the camp. Two of the tents were dark, but the other one had a light in it. I rode up close to it and stopped. I sat there a little bit listening to the talk and laughter coming from inside. Then I hollered, "Anybody home?"

The conversation stopped instantly; then someone shouted, "What the hell was that? It sounded like someone talking; but it CAN'T be. It's nine o'clock at night!"

Then someone stepped out of the tent with a gas lantern. Immediately I recognized the man, a friend of mine, Jack Peters, who took out elk hunters. When Jack saw who it was he announced, "It's that darned game warden! What the hell are YOU doin' ridin' around at this time of night?"

I explained to him that I was on my way back to my cabin. "I just piled my dishes up after breakfast and I have to get back down there and get them washed up."

By this time everybody was outside, and at this point Jack said, "Why don't you stay with us tonight? There's some hot stew in there, and we can rustle up a sleeping bag." I was so glad to hear those words I almost jumped off my horse. I dug my sleeping bag out of the pack and threw it inside the tent where it would warm up. After caring for my horses Jack and I went inside. His hunters were all out of state men who had had limited experience with the great outdoors. They just couldn't understand a person out riding horseback at nine o'clock at night - in a snowstorm, yet! I think they figured that I was ready (or past ready) for the "Funny House". It amazed them that I knew where I was going and could actually get there. Well, as I told them, I KNEW where I wanted to go, and Sally would "see" that I got there.

The next day I was back at the cabin, letting my horses rest. And, I washed the dishes...

Chapter Thirty-Five

One winter in the late '50's the snow piled up deeper than usual which, in turn, drove the elk out of a lot of their winter range. Due to this they did more than average damage to haystacks in my district. Many of us western slope wardens had the same trouble and since we couldn't get enough game fencing to fence against the elk we turned to "night herding" them.

We would drive as close to the stacks as possible, then go from there on snowshoes. I'd been at this effort for about two weeks and as far as I could tell I hadn't gained anything from my endeavor. I had been herding the elk with a 12-gauge shotgun using bird shot to produce a "sting" along with the noise. This wasn't working either. I would run the elk out of the stacks in one field, then go to the next. By the time I'd get back to the first one the elk were right back in that stack yard again! So, I decided to change tactics.

It seemed to me it might work better to let the elk eat for a little while - an hour or two - then go run them out. This way they would back off away from the stacks for a while into the brushy area when I started my herding - and they would browse to finish filling themselves. This appeared to work best.

Sometime it would make me wonder how sane I was. The bottom had dropped out of the thermometer and it turned even more bitterly cold. I was leaving home about midnight, and "herding" until around 4:00 o'clock in the morning. The temperature was a minus 20 to 30 degrees. My wife, Shirley, would see to it that I had a heavy wool scarf to cover most of my face to keep it from freezing. In the long run, however, I think that my efforts helped to pull quite a few elk through the winter and also saved some of the hay for the ranchers. That was one year when I was really glad to see spring arrive.

Elk can live, and even put on weight, while eating hay only, just as cattle do. Deer, however, can make it only if they get some browse in their diet along with the hay. I have fed hundreds of both animals over the years and it can be done successfully if you know how. I learned by trial and error starting back in 1937.

The following winter my activities returned to the norm: I was again "In Pursuit".

In elk country there is always the possibility of poaching. When it occurs in the middle of the winter in areas which are generally inaccessible except on foot or horseback, a game warden faces a particular challenge. So - when the Game Department began using a plane for patrol of such remote regions, among their other uses of the aircraft, the odds became significantly more favorable to my efforts. Up to this time, as I'd followed up on the rumors, I'd met with little success. All that I had accomplished through the extra patrolling both day and night was to develop bags under my eyes.

Since the area I wanted to check was next to impossible to reach on regular patrol I made arrangements to have the plane come up from Grand Junction and fly me over that area. By doing so I was able to orient the pilot to the country where the suspected elk hunting was taking place. This flight was made at the first of the week. Then, I wanted to give it a few days rest without any flights, just in case any of the residents would be a little head-shy of light planes flying overhead.

I played a hunch and scheduled the "air patrol" to come back in and fly the area the following Saturday starting at 10:00 a.m. The pilot was to pass over the designated area and leave. If he didn't find anything he was to buzz me at a given point and go on back to Junction. Then, on Sunday he was to repeat the flight. If he found something, of course, he would contact me by two-way radio and we'd go from there. I would stand by ready to go in on snowshoes if I couldn't reach the spot by 4-wheel drive.

The Saturday flight was made as proposed and nothing out of the ordinary was seen. The pilot buzzed me and headed back to Grand Junction. The rest of the day I spent patrolling several miles away from the "fly-bys" so that I wouldn't be tied in with the plane.

Sunday morning I drove to the airport at 10:00 sharp. Almost immediately I saw the plane come in from the west, up the valley and following the river. As it passed my location the pilot called on the radio and asked if everything was still a "Go". I answered with, "Ten-Four; I will stand by at this point." With binoculars I could see the plane working into the target area, circling occasionally, then flying on.

Suddenly my radio crackled into life with the message, "Car 325, Car 325." I answered with, "Car 325, I read you loud and clear." The pilot continued, "We have a fresh elk kill located, and the hunter is running from the elk to a saddle horse. What do you want us to do now?" My response was, "Get away from there for about ten minutes, then swing back and determine which way the guy is headed. What color are his clothes? What color is the horse? And, is the elk gutted?"

The immediate reply was, "The elk looks like it IS gutted. The horse is black; the man is wearing a brown coat, and has chaps on. Will let you know which way he goes in a little bit." Soaking up this information I headed my pickup toward the scene of action. Some time later I'd reached a high point which enabled me to see most of the country under my current special consideration.

Shortly I saw the plane heading my way; then the pilot called to say that the fellow was heading in the general direction of a ranch, giving its location. "Stand by where you are and we'll make two big dips over the elk carcass so you can pin-point it."

This they did and then reported again on the horsebacker. He was headed "home"! Then, the plane was headed "home".

Meanwhile, I headed to a point about a mile and a half away from the kill and snowshoed into it. I found a four-point bull, shot through the ribs. The hunter had been interrupted by the plane before he had completely gutted the elk; so I finished the job. The bullet had gone clear through the animal; so I would have no evidence for a ballistic test.

I followed the horse trail to within about 300 yards of the ranch, then used ten-power binoculars to determine that the trail led into the corral gate. Four horses were in the corral, and the one eating was as the pilot had described. The other three appeared to be sleeping. I figured the one "balin' hay" was the one that had just returned from some vigorous exercise.

I "webbed" back to my pickup, then drove on up to the ranch. When I knocked on the door there was a long pause before someone jerked the door open. Since we'd met on a former "official" occasion there was little time spent on introductions. Getting right to the point I inquired as to what his activities had been that day before my arrival. He mentioned the usual: he'd fed, then he'd saddled and worked out a horse he was breaking.

To my inquiry as to whether anyone else had been there that day he said that no one had been there but him. "Well, then, I guess you're the man I'm looking for." When I asked him about the elk hair on his coat he explained that it was "off the elk I killed in hunting season".

"Let's go down to the corral and look at this bronc you've been riding," I suggested. In answer to his question as to whether I had a search warrant, I tried to set him straight on the laws in that regard while we were walking to the corral.

The black was still munching hay at the feeder; the others were soaking up what heat they could out of the weak winter sun.

"Which one is the bronc you worked out?" He pointed to the black eating hay. I walked up fairly close to the horse and really looked it over for fresh cinch marks and other saddle marks. I could only see one spot about a half inch long where the cinch ring hadn't been rubbed out. I then asked him what type of saddle he used - single or double rigged. He thought a few seconds and then said, "Double."

"Where do you keep your saddle?"

"In the saddle shed, of course, where else?"

"I want to examine the double rigged saddle you used today." As he opened the tack room door I made a quick look around and saw fresh man tracks leading in and out of an old log cabin. I would have bet right then that the saddle he had used was stashed in the cabin.

We went on in the tack room and he pointed out a saddle supposedly used on the bronc. With just a glance I knew that that saddle hadn't been used for quite some time. There was dried mud on the cinch and the breast collar. At this time of year if any mud was on it, it would be frozen instead of dried.

I turned to him and said, "Let's look at the saddle you hid in the old cabin out there." I was watching his face closely and saw that I had hit pay dirt. Without another word we walked out to the cabin and under a pile of old sacks and saddle blankets, etc. I dug out the saddle I was after. I saw what I was looking for in the stirrups also: caked ice in the bottoms of them, where his feet would rest while riding.

And, in both stirrups the ice was blood-stained, or saturated with blood.

"Well, fella', how do you account for the bloody ice in the stirrups?" I queried. "Shot a rabbit while riding, and I guess I stepped into some of the blood," he replied.

I pulled a pack of cigarettes out of my pocket and removed the cellophane wrapper from the actual container. This makes a small water-proof pouch in a pinch. I then used my pocket knife to shave off some of the bloodiest ice out of the stirrups and dropped it in the little pouch. I held it up before him so he could get a good look at it and said, "Well, I guess you know that the lab in Denver can positively identify this blood; and if the report comes back that it's elk blood, you know what that means."

With that statement he sighed, "Well, I killed the damned elk, and you know it!" He said that there was no use trying to wiggle out of it. It would just cost him a lot of money and he'd lose in the long run. I gave him a summons for illegally killing an elk.

He said that he'd get the elk out in the morning, which he did. He appeared in court as summoned and paid his fine plus costs. This was my last encounter with him.

Chapter Thirty—Six

When I first took over the Meeker-White River district this was where the world's largest mule deer migration was. Many, many thousands of deer would make this trek twice a year between their winter and summer ranges. Especially in the spring of the year during the latter part of April one of my jobs was to get the autos through the deer herds during the peak of the migration. This period lasted about a week and would be heavier during the early morning and late evening.

Without a doubt the fences, especially mesh wire with two or four barbed wires on top made real traps in places. These spots would be searched out and if possible gates were installed in the fences if the land owners would permit so doing. If not, I would tie the barbed wires down to the mesh wire on center between the posts which made for a far less chance of a deer getting its hind legs trapped between two of the barbed wires. Deer that hang up this way usually die a slow death - or they are injured to the point that they have to be destroyed.

This annual heavy migration lasted until the fall of 1948. At this time the biologists in the Game Department brought enough pressure to bear on the Game Commissioners that an either sex season was opened on deer. This was accomplished in spite of heavy opposition from the public. In Meeker, especially, the objection to this decision was great.

It is a proven fact that sentimentalism is a long-term enemy of wildlife. For example, take the bighorn sheep situation in Colorado. For over sixty years the season was kept closed because of public sentimentality. During this time we had heavy die-offs of different sheep herds in Colorado due in part to high concentration.

Heavy die-offs have taken place in various parks in Africa. Tsavo is one of the largest preserves in Africa and reports say that some thirty thousand elephants died off, largely due to sentimentality in one form or another.

At the time of the either-sex season which was proposed for the fall of 1948, I was guilty of this sentimentalism, too; however not to the point that most White River residents were. Down deep within myself I knew that something would have to be done - either a very generous hunting season - or, Mother Nature would take strict measures, no doubt in the form of a very hard winter, causing a massive die-off.

At that time the area east of Meeker, for roughly twenty five miles - was winter elk range, without any deer wintering throughout this area. Likewise, west of Meeker, clear to the Utah line, it was all deer range. For years I never saw a trace of an elk being west of Highway 13 between Meeker and Rifle and west of the Strawberry Creek road which runs north of Meeker to the Moffat County line.

I felt sure - and in a short time was proven right - that if either-sex deer hunting was permitted east of Meeker numerous old does would be killed leaving their fawns in the area. Some of the fawns would migrate down with the main migration and some would winter kill; but, nevertheless, there would be some that would make it through the winter - in the only territory they knew - and where they would remain.

The fawns that did make it through the winter would stay and raise their fawns here in the same area, and, in a few short years there would be a buildup of a non-migrating deer herd that would run competition with the elk for food and, in tough winters they would be subject to a die-off from starvation.

This very thing that I had feared did happen and today there are non-migrating deer east of Meeker in the Oak Ridge area and along the White River road leading up to the Buford area.

Eventually this action had a large part to play in the demise of the big trophy bucks of White River because of post seasons. Of course, other factors coupled with the post seasons helped accomplish the kill of the big bucks; but I think the post seasons played the biggest role. Those post seasons were liberal and took place during the rut. The trophy-sized bucks that were able to elude most hunters during the regular season fell easy prey during the rut. They seemed almost blind to everything except a doe in heat. Also, they were out traveling around all day, so they were much easier to locate by hunters.

As this is being written it is hard to find a trophy-sized buck in the White River country. I know; I try every year, and for the past five years I haven't killed a buck because I haven't been able to find a big one.

I feel sure that had the either-sex hunting season been held only west of Meeker we would have retained a deer migration similar to what it used to be, and the buck census wouldn't be in the sad state it is today.

We also have to admit to the human influences which have affected the deer's habitat. An invading population, added roads, travel and construction of various kinds are all factors. And, perhaps the growing protection of predators has a bearing on the situation as well.

Chapter Thirty-Seven

One winter after moving to Meeker in 1947, the snow piled up and the temperature dropped down to where the red stuff turned blue, and it didn't warm up much throughout the day. Over in Moffat County in the antelope area it snowed and blew most of the brush under to the point the animals couldn't find much to eat. By February they were getting in bad shape and had started moving south.

They were bunching up against the highway fence along U.S. 40 just east of Elk Springs. Some of the last spring's fawns were beginning to die from malnutrition and the extremely cold weather.

Bill Roland, the warden at Craig in whose district this was happening, alerted our mutual boss and asked for some help to move the antelope south across highway 40. So, Cleve called me explaining the situation and said that I should get my snowshoes ready. He would pick me up in the morning and we'd meet Bill in Craig, continuing on down to Elk Springs and see what could be done.

The next morning we arrived at Elk Springs to see antelope by the hundreds bunched up against the highway fence - and more were coming for as far as you could see them. It didn't take us long to get the operation in gear. Men from the State Highway Department were standing by to give us a hand.

The plan we had decided on was to plow a trail from the north fence across the highway right-of-way, through the south fence line and up to a brush-covered ridge south of the highway.

The Highway Department had a D-8 dozer on hand, and some of their men would stop the traffic (there wasn't much in those days) so the antelope could cross over to the south side. While this was being done Bill, another fellow and I snowshoed north, around most of the herd, then started pushing them with loud whoops and hollers.

They didn't need much encouragement to get them started across the highway. Soon I found a little fawn (last spring's) that was completely worn out and just wouldn't, couldn't go any further. I picked the little guy up and carried him in my arms. I had a wool coat on and I guess this warmed the little fellow.

After we'd gone just a short distance he made no more effort to try and get away from me. When I reached the road most of the antelope were pretty well worked across. I set the fawn down, expecting him to follow the last ones that crossed. To my surprise, though, he didn't want to leave me! I pushed him away two or three times and tried to get away from him on my snowshoes.

He followed me to the top of the ridge and near to the other antelope. I decided that the only way to get away from him - or him from me - as the case seemed to be, was to head out into the deep snow. This idea worked. As I webbed down over the ridge towards the highway the little fawn was just starting to follow the herd.

There were some of these antelope that worked south to as far as Highway 64 south of White River. A few head even worked up to Yellow Creek which was several miles east of where they first hit White River. And, in June of 1987, a buck antelope was seen by golfers on the Meeker golf course. Where he came from no one would ever know.

I often wondered, though, what ever became of the little fawn that I carried up to the ridge on that cold and snowy morning so many years ago.

Chapter Thirty-Eight

On the morning of September 9, 1972, Fred LeTendre, my Yukon guide, and I tied the finish knot on the diamond hitch on the second pack horse we were taking along. I marveled at this easy-going man who never seemed to hurry, but got things done "muy pronto".

As I slipped my model 70 Winchester into the saddle scabbard Fred was giving last minute instructions to the balance of the "men in charge" and I heard him tell the guide who would be left as Number One Boy that we would be back day after tomorrow. I thought, "day after tomorrow!" would mean a tight schedule even with fairly good luck.

Around mid-morning we had topped out on the mountain range south of our base camp which was nestled alongside the Nisling River. As we searched the country ahead of us with binoculars I picked up a light-colored object that immediately moved out of sight behind some heavy brush a good mile distant. As I pointed out the location to Fred he swung his binoculars to bear on the spot. About the same time the light spot reappeared, and Fred exclaimed, "Grizzly!". That word, spoken that way, especially in grizzly country automatically draws the attention of the hunter.

At this point three more smaller spots appeared around the larger one. It turned out to be an old sow and three spring cubs. We watched them through our glasses and the spotting scope until they worked their way up and over the ridge, all the while turning logs and rocks over as they went, looking for bugs and ants. Those three cubs seemed to be everywhere at once and full of the devil. I've always enjoyed watching bear cubs play.

The balance of the day was spent hunting to the south. We checked over several small herds of caribou, but none of the bulls were good enough to draw our fire.

About an hour before dark we pitched our camp along a small creek where there was plenty of grass for the horses and dry fire wood for camp. The horses were hobbled, except for Fred's saddle horse which was picketed by a front foot. When supper was over we sat around the camp fire until the stars came out. All the time we were swapping tales of the past; Fred was full of very interesting information about British Columbia and the Yukon. Part of the success of any hunt - from rabbits to grizzlies - is good companionship as well as the great outdoors that you are enjoying. The older I get the more I realize how important these two factors are.

The wood smoke from a campfire, the tinkle of the horse bells and the stars in the sky have always put my mind and soul at ease.

Next morning after a hearty breakfast we picketed the two pack horses near camp, then headed out towards the south. The idea was to make a huge circle, winding up at camp towards evening.

By mid-afternoon we had seen quite a lot of grizzly sign and we also saw several small bunches of caribou. Two different bulls were considered; however, upon closer examination we passed them up.

Toward evening as we headed down a wide long ridge toward the headwaters of the creek our camp was on Fred suddenly pulled his horse to a stop and pointed to the right. Two big bull caribou had popped up as if by magic and were standing there looking at us!

As I quit the saddle, snaking the Magnum from the scabbard, I turned in time to see the bulls trot out of sight behind some scrub evergreens. We quickly tied our horses to some brush and hot-footed it to the edge of the ridge. Both bulls looked good; the leader had a very wide shovel and the rest of the head was mighty fine. They were quartering slightly to the left at about 150 yards; I didn't have time to take anything but an off hand shot. It was now or never; so, I laid the cross hairs just back of the shoulder for a forward raking shot, swung with the bull and "touched 'er off". As the sharp crack of the Magnum shattered the Yukon stillness I saw the bull pitch forward on his nose.

Starting over to where the bull piled up, Fred said, "I'll be damned! Look up there at those rascals!" I took a quick look in the direction he was pointing and to my amazement I saw three grizzlies loping along, wide open, for the top of the hill above them. No doubt they had been bushed up in the creek bottom below the caribou and my shot scared them out. All three were two-year-old cubs, large; but not big enough to be trophies. We watched them disappear over the ridge. A grizzly going full-tilt can cover ground rapidly.

After caping out the trophy and taking some pictures we took what meat we could handle and prepared the balance for pickup tomorrow with the pack horses.

For supper that evening we stuffed ourselves with biscuits, honey and roasted caribou ribs. They are almost as good as roasted sheep ribs. The next day we would pick up the balance of the meat and hunt back to our main camp on the Nisling River, hopefully finding a good grizzly along the way.

Chapter Thirty-Nine

When I picked up Jim Findlay, the Cattlemen's Association deputy, at his home in Meeker one Sunday I planned on spending the day patrolling the Little Beaver Creek area. By the middle of the afternoon we had worked out a lot of this area and hadn't contacted too many hunters. Due to this I told Jim that I thought we would work up Coal Creek to Sleepy Cat Mountain, over to Cow Creek, back down to White River, then on into Meeker.

We checked one camp that had a bull elk on the meat pole, then next on our swing around Sleepy Cat, we found that someone had decided to camp in a deserted cabin.

We drove over to the cabin, saw a Model A Ford

parked nearby, but no visible signs of "residents". I knocked on the door - no answer; couldn't raise anyone. So, I headed back to my pickup. Walking back, though, I happened to notice a white cotton meat sack hanging out of the left hand window of the old Ford. It was still plenty light enough to notice that there were blood stains on the sack. Then, looking through the car window I could see the remains of a hind quarter of deer lying on a brown paper sack on the floorboards.

Motioning Jim over to see what I'd found, I said, "Let's look around here a little bit more and see if we can find the rest of that deer." Jim went one way, I the other. I expected to find the deer hanging in a tree south of the cabin, so I started to follow a path leading out into the timber. Suddenly I saw someone slipping along the path towards me. At first I thought maybe it was Jim; but, no, it couldn't be; he was wearing a broad-brimmed hat; this fellow had on a cap.

It was beginning to get dusk and up to this time I hadn't noticed that the guy was holding a rifle hip-high and pointed right at me. Suddenly he was less than a hundred feet from me. I immediately stepped off the path and behind a pine tree. I hollered loud enough that he could certainly hear me and asked him to point the rifle at the ground and approach me before someone got hurt. He hesitated a minute, then walked over to me. By that time Jim had heard the loud talk and he showed up.

I told the man who we were and suggested that we go back to the cabin where it was warmer and where we might have better light. When I asked him about the deer meat he denied any knowledge of it -

didn't know of any deer meat around. He was hunting elk and didn't have a deer license. Before we reached the cabin I asked him if there was anyone with him; he said, "No" - he was alone.

Back at the cabin he opened the door and invited us in. As soon as I stepped through the door I could smell the odor of cooked fresh meat. My mind returned to the deer meat in the old Ford. Meanwhile, I noticed that there was an iron skillet on the back of the wood-burning stove. So - just on a hunch I lifted the lid and looked in the skillet. It came as no surprise that there were three or four small pieces of fried meat still in it.

I turned around to the man and said, "It looks like you've had some fresh steak today." All at once the fellow said to Jim and me, "Look, Men, I'm a preacher, and if I don't tell you the truth the devil will get me!" I responded, "Well, Mister, it looks like the devil's already gotcha'."

Then he told us that he had killed the old doe for camp meat two days ago. When I asked him what he had done with the rest of the meat he said that it was hanging back in the trees for future use.

I pulled out my summons book and told the preacher that I was going to write him a ticket for possession of illegal deer meat.

Seated at a rickety table, I began writing his summons, while the parson seemed to be in deep thought. All of a sudden he leaped up off of the stool he'd been sitting on, extended his arms outward with palms up and exclaimed excitedly, "Hold it, Men! HOLD IT!"

Needless to say, this brought Jim and me "to" in a split second and we both jumped up immediately, standing there in a state of complete dismay. We didn't know WHAT was coming next!

Then, in a reverent tone he asked, "Have you Boys been SAVED yet?" I replied, "Well, I guess. At least I'm here." Jim just stared - first at him, then at me - with a nondescript expression on his face.

Again, the man of the cloth offered, "I can SAVE you Boys!" Continuing, "Now, why don't you both just sit down over there while I preach you a sermon?" I countered with, "I think it might be best right now if you'd concentrate on saving yourself."

With Sunday evening services over - I returned to my completion of his summons, handed it to him and urged that he join us at the courthouse in Meeker the next day at 10:00 a.m.

Jim and I gathered up the deer meat and headed for Meeker. As we reached town Jim concluded that, once again as my partner, he had experienced another one-of-a-kind-day and was ready for 'supper and some shut-eye".

Good idea...

Chapter Forty

It was July when I decided to pack some fry-sized native trout up to two different lakes I had found on the Flat Tops. At the time I discovered them they were unnamed and were situated off the main trail which was used by horsebackers who rode the Flat Tops from end to end.

After I'd found these two small lakes I spent several days checking them for depth, fresh water inlets, apparent food, water temperature, average year-around water level and, the outlets. After studying all of this data I concluded that it would be worth the effort to pack some stocker fish up there.

In those days if a game warden found waters that didn't contain fish, and he thought the waters would sustain them, he could go ahead and try to raise trout in them. This was several years before the advent of stocking the high lakes, and other waters, by airplane. Also, it was before we started using plastic two-gallon jugs filled approximately three-fourths full of water, then adding the very small fish - "fry", or first stage fingerlings. The balance of the space was pumped full of pure oxygen.

That wasn't the case earlier. Then, we had to use either five or ten gallon cream cans to hold the small stocker fish and the water necessary to transport them. The lids of these cans were cut out and a very fine mesh wire was installed to permit air to enter and mix with the water that was sloshing around due to the movement of the horses packing them. We'd use two cans per pack horse, one can lashed to each side of the horse.

On a long pack trip quite often we would use the larger ten-gallon cans which permitted more water for the fish. Even then, on days when it was very hot, we would have to change the water before reaching our destination when we found colder water. This meant unpack the cream cans, change the water in them and then repack the cans.

When I decided to stock these two lakes I had to put in my order for the number of fry trout to be delivered to me at the South Fork campground on a certain day. I then tried to find a man to help me with the packing, but couldn't find anyone who wanted to earn a few dollars that way. The fish had been ordered from the Glenwood Springs hatchery; the order was confirmed and I was obligated to go through with my idea. This order was for fifteen hundred fry native trout; so I would have to use two ten-gallon cans, dividing the fish between the two cans.

9:30 a m. with the little trout. I'd hauled my saddle horse and a pack horse up to the campground the evening before. Since I was alone, the driver of the fish truck helped me get the cans on the pack saddle and lashed down good for the ride up to the Flat Tops. This trip would take about four hours of steady riding. I knew that I would have to change the water before I reached my destination; so when I got to Lost Solar Creek I decided to change the water. When I checked the fish they were in good shape. This is where the real work came in. After getting the ten-gallon cans full of water and the fish up onto the pack saddle they had to be lashed down. This done, I continued on up to the Flat Tops.

When I arrived at the first lake I had to unpack both cans, of course. Having divided the number of fish into the two cans I poured one can of little fish into the first lake, then refilled the can with water so it would balance the load until I reached the other lake. I unloaded both cans, again, dumped the rest of the fish in the second lake - then repacked two empty cans and headed down country to my cabin where I spent the night.

The last time I fished these lakes the fish were doing fine. They averaged about fifteen inches in length. Several years later, after I'd stocked these lakes the first time, they were stocked by plane. That was quite a difference - no comparison between the two methods - and so much easier the second time around!

Some Texas people found these two lakes and named one "Lard Lake" and the other one "Elk Lake". Whether they still go by these names I have no idea.

Along in August I returned to the Top to check the lakes and maybe see some elk. About two miles from the first lake I got a snoot-full of wood smoke since the wind was in my face. I was cutting through the scattered pines and windfalls on a straight line for that first lake.

Soon I saw several saddle horses and one pack horse, all tied to trees dead ahead. My horse had her ears pointed forward even before I saw the tied horses. She didn't whinny at the horses. I never remember Sally ever whinnying at another horse while under the saddle. This fact permitted me to ride up to within ten or twelve feet of a huge pine tree that had blown down several years before. Immediately on the other side of the tree was a campfire, with a big coffee pot shoved into the red embers. There were about nine people sitting around.

My horse stopped and I just leaned forward to rest my elbows on the pommel. While I was sitting there listening to the conversation one fellow looked and saw me sitting there. Min Beard's first words were, "Why don't you get down and join the party?"

A lady sitting just across from the big tree turned around, looked up and saw me. I knew Vivian, and her husband, Dr. Alexander. I stepped off my horse and joined them for a cup of coffee. Vivian just couldn't believe that anyone could ride up that close to them and not be heard. From then on she always swore that I had "rubber shoes" on my horse.

They had been fishing and were on their way back to the South Fork campground when they decided to have a late lunch and a cup of java. (To a non-coffee drinker it had quite a kick to it; but the invitation was most welcome, and the company was great, for sure!)

Incidentally, Vivian is an expert in bugling like a bull elk. She doesn't use a device of any kind - just her throat and cupped hands. She fooled me once for about four bugles. (Her tutor was E.D.J. Stevens - also known as "Alphabetical Steve" - who was one of the best buglers ever.)

Then - it was time for me to continue the patrol to my pet lakes and the surrounding area.

Chapter Forty-One

As time went on reports and other paper work increased which, in turn, forced the game warden to spend more time in his "office" getting this unwanted job done.

One day during the latter part of deer season I had to spend some time on reports; so elected to get them out that evening if possible. Then, I would patrol until around midnight.

Toward evening I received a call from Guy Post who operated Sleepy Cat Lodge; he said that I was needed there urgently. Well, I jumped at this welcome interruption of office work!

The lodge was only about a mile from my home; so I was soon there. When I asked what service I might render I was told that a hunter had taken a fawn a couple of hours earlier, and "stored it in the trunk of his sedan", then driven to the lodge for supper. When I was introduced to the hunter he said that the deer was still alive and kicking up quite a fuss in the car. I could imagine!

Upon going out to his car I found that he had TWO FAWNS! He had captured them in a woven wire fence corner. When he caught them he tried to tie the feet together on one of the fawns, then put it in the trunk. Next, he "hog-tied" the other one and - PUT IT IN THE BACK SEAT!

By the time he arrived at the lodge things were getting quite lively in the car. The fawn inside was making a grand mess of things, while the one in the trunk was more subdued. Both had gotten their feet loose.

I first opened the trunk lid and that fawn came out of there jet-propelled! I immediately opened the car door on the side toward the direction the "trunked" fawn had taken off so they could "pair up" again.

When asked what he planned to do with the two fawns he said, "Take 'em home to the kids for pets." I just imagine that he'd had all of the "Bambies" and "Bring 'em Back Alive" he wanted for a long time.

Well, that was only the beginning! Then I was called DOWN the river - to patrol south of Meeker.

I caught up with a station wagon and immediately realized that something was wrong with the driver. He was slouched over the steering wheel and was zig-zagging back and forth all over the road. After stopping him I found that he'd indulged considerably over his capacity. He'd had several too many for the road.

He had been hunting and had shot an old doe, which was illegal, and he'd managed to trap a fawn in a fence, tied it up and dumped it in the back of the station wagon along with the ungutted deer!

Since he was in no condition to gut the doe - I did. And, of course, turned the fawn loose. Then, after seizing the doe, I took the keys from the ignition to keep him from trying to drive.

At that time of night in those days there wasn't much travel on the roads in that area. I called the highway patrolman on my two-way radio and he soon arrived on the scene, to deal with the drunk-driving situation.

The hunter had to appear in J.P. court the next day to answer to the game law violation that I had lodged against him, at which time the Judge asked him just what he intended to do with the live fawn? He replied that he planned on taking it back to his home in a southern state and cross it with a white-tailed deer there "to make a bigger and healthier animal". An insurmountable task in my estimation.

The Judge fined him $150.00 and costs, then gave him a lecture on driving under the influence and let him be on his way - without his "breeding stock" - I might add!

And, I still had reports to do!

Well, my account of THIS evening's activities should bring a smile to my supervisor's face...

Chapter Forty-Two

Several years ago I drew a muzzleloader elk license. An archer friend of mine, Frank Hulce from Hawaii, was here to hunt with bow and arrow, and had been hunting for about a week by the time muzzleloader season opened. Frank wanted to hunt with me with the idea that if we should get a shot at a bull within thirty-five yards he would take it, and any shot over thirty-five yards I should take with the muzzleloader.

Frank is an expert at bugling; so I figured that this would be a good combination. I was going to hunt with a .54 caliber "Smoke Pole" which I'd built over the last two winters during my spare time. This rifle turned out to be quite accurate at all ranges up to 130 yards with a load of 100 grains of Pyrodex R.S. and a 425 grain Great Plains conical bullet.

Opening morning of the muzzleloader season found Frank and me hunting up through the timber which was a mixture of pine and aspen. Just as we entered a park with a few scattered aspen - a bull elk bugled ahead of us. It sounded to be about 300 to 400 yards away. We concealed ourselves in some low evergreen cover, then Frank returned the bugle. After waiting for about ten minutes - nothing happened; so, we continued on.

Just before we were to enter a finger of pines I noticed a movement out of the corner of my eye, off to the right and a little below us. It was a nice heavy-horned five-point bull about fifty yards away - standing broadside to us. The thought flashed through my mind that this bull was as good as on the meat pole back at camp! Since there was a big aspen tree right beside me I eased the hammer back on the muzzle-loader, leaned up against the aspen, got the peep sight full of elk ribs and squeezed the trigger. Instead of a roar and a cloud of gray smoke that I expected, there was just a loud "bang". Only the cap fired, but not the load!

As I dug into my pocket for another cap the bull started to walk off, so Frank bugled at him and he stopped, again broadside. By this time I had recapped and leaned against the aspen - once more I drew a bead on his ribs and squeezed the trigger. I got the same results from the rifle as before! This time the bull walked into the pines in spite of the calls Frank made.

Right then and there I pulled the load out and cleaned the nipple and channel. Then I reloaded, popped another cap on the nipple, pointed the old "coal burner" at the aspen and pulled the trigger.

There was the expected recoil, roar and cloud of smoke! That was an embarrassing experience - and a good lesson. I have heard and read many times to be sure that the nipple and channel are clean before going afield.

In the fall of 1991, I drew a muzzleloader license again. For the past three or four years I had done a lot of practice with my rifle, especially off-hand shooting up to 150 yards. So, when the season rolled around in '91 I was ready.

Taking a light lunch I headed for my hunting area to pit my skills against that of the bull elk. At about 11:00 a.m. I picked up the tracks of maybe a dozen head of elk traveling into the wind and paralleling the top of the mountain where I was hunting. By 11:30 the tracks indicated the elk were feeding a little and would no doubt bed down soon for the middle of the day. Also I knew that within the next hour the wind or breeze could change directions under this mountain top. If and when that happened the elk would get my wind and that would be the end of hunting this little herd for the day. I hoped the herd would bed down as their tracks indicated before they traveled too much farther.

At this point I climbed out on top of the mountain, worked over to the other side where I could glass some big parks and eat my lunch. Since this was actually on the other side of the mountain I didn't think it possible for the elk to get wind of me even if the wind changed in their favor.

After eating my lunch I worked along the mountain for several hundred yards, then eased up on top to find that the breeze had changed directions and now was blowing westward. I dropped down into the edge of the timber and immediately caught the musky smell of elk. As I inched forward I saw two or three cows, a calf and then a four-point bull stepped into an opening between two pines. The next step put his front quarters behind a pine. I cocked my rifle as I carefully took a step to my right. That exposed his right side. There was no time to study the situation; the rifle butt hit my shoulder, the sights settled for an instant on his ribs and I squeezed the trigger. There was a blast - and a huge cloud of smoke blotted out the scene before me. I heard the "thunk" of the bullet hitting; then there was mass confusion of elk crashing through the timber. Right then I didn't know what had happened to the bull; started reloading as the smoke cleared.

I walked over to where the bull was when I shot. At first I couldn't find hair, blood or any indication of a hit. Then, as I followed his tracks for about twenty yards to an outcropping of slide rock I found a big splotch of blood. At the bottom of the slide I found the bull - piled up against a big rock. This was about sixty yards from where he was when I shot.

Upon gutting him I found the minie ball had entered about the middle of the ribs, took out an inch of one rib, passed through both lungs, went through another rib and finally lodged against the hide on the left side. The ball was mushroomed to twice its ordinary size. I opened him up so he would cool out and then headed back to camp. The following day I got five of the archery hunters to go back with me and help pack the meat back to camp.

This time my rifle was clean - and it fired like it should have - instead of like it did on the first time I tried to shoot an elk with it. Without a doubt these muzzleloaders will get the job done if the shooter does his part. In other words, keep your gun clean! And, do a lot of practice with it.

Know your gun and its capabilities, as well as your own.

Chapter Forty-Three

Each spring the Department held a "Game Management" meeting; and in the fall, just before hunting season, we had a "Law Enforcement" meeting. These gatherings afforded all of the personnel an opportunity to become informed regarding policies and regulations. In addition, these times provided forums for the exchange of views and recommendations which the employees thought were worthy of consideration.

I have always felt that sooner or later most individuals, regardless of their employment, will have an idea which they would like to see become a reality. I, for one, certainly have entertained a number of such ideas. Some have been implemented; others have fallen by the wayside. One example is regarding my design for a big game license. Having in mind what I considered improvements, I prepared a sample and presented it at one of our inner-Department meetings.

One particular feature of the license was the carcass tag; information on the tag included the date and sex of the animal, and was to be punched, or cut, out at the time of the kill.

During a break I showed it to my regional boss and explained what I considered to be the advantages of the design. Then, after lunch he came before the group and held my sample up for view of all in attendance, and gave a brief explanation of it. There seemed to be a general agreement that it was probably a good idea, but it was doubtful that it would ever work for reasons too numerous to mention.

Now Colorado and a large number of other states have developed a concept of big game licenses on the order of my sample.

Another proposal I had which I think "stands tall in the saddle" is the adoption of a practice to protect the spike bull elk. This has been one of my main causes for several years.

I first became concerned with this issue when the branch antlered bull ratio fell to about two or three per one hundred cows. It doesn't take a super smart person to see the trouble with this ratio. Oh, sure, some spikes will breed cows, but the calf produced stands a very good chance of being inferior to a calf sired by a mature bull.

For several years it occurred that about 82% to 87% of the bulls killed in the White River country were spikes (18 months old). I personally don't know of any ranchers that use 18-month olds as herd bulls.

In addition to this, no hunter looking for a trophy is going to take a spike. The only way to achieve larger bulls would be either close the season in certain areas or put an antler point restriction on them. There was no question that something had to be done, and soon.

I decided to pursue this matter with great vigor. An idea started forming in my mind sometime after the mid-'50's. From then on everytime I had a chance I'd bring up the protection of spike bulls, but it didn't appear to make much impression. I was once told that the Department couldn't afford to carry over from one year to the next any surplus of spikes. The reason given was that the Department needed the money from the license sales on elk. I figured a way in my own mind to "have your cake and eat part of it, too", so to speak.

My idea was to go back over the last five years' records and determine the number of spikes taken each season. After obtaining these figures, take an average for the five years, then cut that average number in half. Protect one-half of the spikes and put the other half on a permit system, drawing for the permit the same as is done with antlerless elk.

When I submitted this idea at a management meeting I was informed that it wouldn't work for several reasons. One main objection was that it would be too expensive to set up a drawing system for the spike permits. I came back at them with the fact that special draws were in effect, and had been for some time, for other game animals such as bighorn sheep, antelope and cow elk. By using the permit system on spike elk they could protect some of the little bulls so they could grow into the branch antlered category and, at the same time, be able to take in some money from the sale of the other half of the number. When my proposal was turned down flat I saw that I would have to attack the matter from a different angle.

After I retired I watched the bull elk situation continue to deteriorate. In the following two or three years it became almost impossible to find a branch-antlered bull. Unless you were lucky enough to draw a cow elk permit your chances of getting an elk were few and far between unless you took the first spike you could find.

Finally, I was able to enlist sympathetic ears in the Game and Fish Commission through Commissioner Dr. Wilton W. Cogswell, Jr. who agreed with me in principle. When I had explained my views, reasons therefore, and suggested my ideas on the matter it was concluded that I had some beneficial solutions which were worthy of consideration. After so long a time the Commissioners were persuaded to see the situation in the same light and that fall spikes were on the protected list. "Hot Dingies!". There was a "toe-hold".

The next fall a legal bull had to have two or more points on one horn to be legal. Even after one season it was evident that protecting the spikes had helped considerably. Then - we went right back to making ALL bulls legal.

Later on, the point system was established again. Then it was necessary for a bull to have at least four points on one antler to be legal. Now, years later, it is obvious that the "point system" on antlers is working. I hope that it will be kept in effect for years to come.

In this book you have seen the picture of a bull head that I took many, many years ago. It took a spike a long time to grow a head which scores as this one does, 400 0/8 points in the Boone and Crockett Club records.

Chapter Forty-Four

The winter of 1964-65 was a cold, tough one on deer and elk. As the snow piled up it covered a lot of the brush that supplied food for all of these animals. In addition, the deep snow made travel much more difficult for them, especially the deer. Elk can handle much deeper snow than the deer can.

Hay for livestock was in heavy demand and a lot of it was being hauled out of areas that grew large quantities of it, trucking it to less productive locations. And now the weather conditions were forcing the deer and elk down to the haystacks, causing considerable damage to the stacks and loss of hay the ranchers needed desperately for their livestock, or to sell for transport to other areas.

This situation became so bad that, in fact, one elk was seen just outside the Meeker city limits, and numerous deer were feeding on pawed-out apples and decorative shrubs in yards in town.

The heavy depredation on the haystacks caused an above average run on game fencing. Most of this was used to fence out elk, and with the demand so great, each district wound up having employees build panels from material furnished by the Game Department.

Due to the heavy workload of building and delivering the elk panels to ranches that needed them I fell behind on patrolling my district which included Piceance Creek, mainly a deer area. There were some elk wintering in the tributaries to the creek, however. By February the deer had lost, or used up, all of their fat and now they were very skinny. In addition, they were congregating along the Piceance Creek road where they could feed on any available brush.

Over the past month I had mentioned to the new supervisor that I felt I should be doing more patrolling and less game fence building. Each time I brought up this subject he told me that the old-fashioned idea of patrolling all the time was far less important than getting the elk panels built. I would come back with the fact that he could hire someone to build panels but he couldn't go out and hire just anyone to do the patrolling. Unfortunately, I wasn't giving the orders; so, I continued to build panels.

Shortly after lunch one day a couple of men drove up to the panel-building yard with a flat-bed truck to get a load of elk panels. They were from Piceance Creek and while one of them was busy talking with some of the other Department men around, the other fellow called me aside. We walked around to the far side of the truck out of earshot of the others and he said to me, "Bill, have you been down on the Creek lately?" I said, "No, why?" "Just yesterday," he replied, "I was going up to Rio Blanco and came around a turn just below the mouth of Thirteen Mile where there were two guys standing on the side of the road, shooting at an old doe and two fawns - last spring's fawns." He said that they didn't pay much attention to him; they had a truckload of hay and at first he just supposed that they were trying to get some venison. After mulling it over on the balance of the trip to Rio Blanco, though, he decided that anyone after a piece of venison wouldn't want a skinny old doe for meat; something else must be the reason.

While shootin' the bull at Rio Blanco he was told by another Piceance Creek man that he, too, had caught some of the hay-haulers shooting at deer on two different occasions. They got to comparing notes and found that it was the same truck and, apparently, the same men that each of them had seen shooting at the deer. He said that he didn't mind anyone getting some meat; but he couldn't go for just shooting the deer and leaving them. I assured him that I would never give out his name and that I would be down the next day to check things out.

After these men left with their load of game fencing I contacted my supervisor and told him what I had learned. He had no choice but to give me the O.K. to drop my part of panel-building and go down on Piceance Creek to look things over.

The next morning on my way to the upper end of Piceance I stopped in at the Rio Blanco store to see if I could pick up any more information. I slid up to the counter and ordered a cup of hot chocolate to sip on, hoping to gather more details. I'd been there about five minutes when a hay-haulers' truck turned down Piceance Creek. I was passing the time of day with a store "regular" who spent quite a bit of time hanging around the place. I asked him if that was one of the trucks hauling hay out of the area. He said that it was and they'd been hauling for about three weeks now.

"Are you goin' down the crick, Bill?" I nodded that I was, and said that I thought it was about time that I did. "Tom" looked around to see that no one was close by, then said, in a low voice, "Bill, someone is shootin' deer just for the HELL of it! They ain't takin' the meat, and I don't like it! I think ya' might find somethin' if ya' really look the area over." I finished my chocolate and headed down the "crick". By now I predicted that the trip would prove most interesting!

From Rio Blanco west to White River it's forty-five miles with some large side streams coming into the main Piceance Creek. A lot of hay is produced in this area. (It's said that "Piceance" in the Ute language means "Tall Grass".)

First, I wanted to find out where the hay-haulers were hauling from. About two-thirds of the way down the creek I located two trucks; one was the outfit I'd seen turn down the creek while I was at Rio Blanco. Both trucks were being loaded with hay.

I drove down to the mouth of Dry Fork where I turned around and headed back up. I wanted to look for empty cartridge cases and also let the haulers get out of the area. I preferred they didn't see me investigating anything at that point. I'd seen several places with two or three dead deer off to the side of the road. I wanted to check these out on my way back up to the store.

Along this stretch of road a deer is hit and killed by a car every once in a while. These deer, thrown off the road, didn't interest me as far as an examination went. I pulled out to a point where I could use my binoculars to watch the hay-haulers and there I ate my lunch.

About 12:30 the fellows had loaded up and pulled out, headed back to Rio Blanco. This is what I was waiting for. Now I would have the rest of the day to scout for dead deer.

A mile or so up the road from where the hay was being hauled I found some empty .22 cartridges. Then I really started looking this area over. The afternoon produced seven deer that had been shot with small caliber bullets. All of the dead deer were does and fawns.

The amazing thing I found was the fact that on all seven animals the bullets had gone clear through. It was hard to believe that an ordinary .22 caliber bullet, even the .22 long rifle, would shoot clear through a deer at 75 to 125 yards. All seven had been hit within that distance as indicated by their tracks in the snow. I wondered if the deer were being shot with a .22 Magnum since it's considerably more powerful than the ordinary .22. However, the fact that the deer were exceptionally thin lent them to less resistance to the bullets, permitting the bullets to penetrate their bodies completely. I had to find deer that the bullet or bullets were lodged in; the ones I'd found where the bullets had passed completely through didn't help much. And, try as I did, I couldn't find any empty cases except for regular .22's; but there were plenty of them!

None of the deer I found had been shot near a haystack; so, I couldn't come up with any logical reason as to why they were shot - other than that the person or persons responsible were doing it just because they had a craze to shoot something.

I had begun this investigation in February; now, on the 16th day of March I had found a total of thirty-nine deer that had been shot with what appeared to be a .22 caliber. Without a doubt this was only a very small percentage of the deer that had actually been shot. Probably no greater than five or six percent were found, as a .22 bullet through the body would permit most of the victims to get up into the cedars on the mountains before they died.

I spent from about daylight 'til dark checking this area and gaining all of the information I could for several weeks, and long before I'd found the 39th deer carcass I had vowed to get the person or persons doing the killing and wasting the deer.

Eventually, I found four deer that had the bullets still lodged in them. One was so "ripe", however, that I couldn't trace the wound after the bullet had entered the body. From the other three I was able to dig out four bullets. All were .22 long rifle slugs.

Now that I had the bullets I needed the guns they were fired from. If I could get the guns I would take them and the bullets to Denver and get ballistic tests of them. Although I suspected the hay-haulers, a lot of people on White River carried guns in their vehicles so there was always the possibility that someone else was the trigger-happy individual.

During my investigations on Piceance Creek I had been seen several times by the hay-haulers. Due to this I figured that if they WERE the gunners they would halt their shooting immediately and leave their guns at home. This made even more sense, too, when I could find no more fresh kill anywhere along the Piceance Creek road.

Suspecting the hay-haulers was not enough, though. I would still have to have their guns for the ballistic tests. So, I decided to see if I could enlist the help of a local Highway Patrolman. Since he was a State officer he had the right to obtain the information I needed. He could check the haulers' loads and at the same time he could get their names and addresses.

In a couple of days I had the names and addresses of three men. Next, I had to know what days these men did not haul hay. This information was provided by sources down on the Creek. Then, I would need three teams of two men each to make searches of these haulers' homes to try and find the guns used to shoot the deer. I needed five officers besides myself to make up the teams. I got the teams lined up through my supervisor and then obtained the necessary search warrants from the Deputy District Attorney, George E. Benner, Jr.

The following morning we hit all of the targets at the same time so one party couldn't warn the next one of the searches. The objects of our searches were 22 caliber guns. Of the three places searched we came up with one .22 caliber six-shooter and three .22 rifles.

My next step was to take the guns and bullets retrieved from the deer carcasses out to the police lab in Denver for ballistic exams. The tests established the fact that one of the rifles and the six-shooter had been used to shoot the deer that the bullets came from.

Complaints and warrants for arrest were issued and the two owners of the guns were served. They appeared before Rio Blanco County Judge Keith Dunbar in Meeker in separate trials and both were found guilty.

Unfortunately, there was nothing I could do about the other thirty-five head that I'd found which had been shot. Since the bullets had completely penetrated their bodies I had no proof of anyone's guilt of shooting them.

This case proved to be one of my more challenging ones, and was a fitting conclusion to my career In Pursuit as a law officer for the Colorado Division of Wildlife.

I retired May 1, 1965.

"Over and Out!"